Middlemarch and the Imperfect Life

Middlemarch
and the Imperfect Life

BOOKMARKED

PAMELA ERENS

New York, NY

Ig Publishing
Box 2547
New York, NY 10163
www.igpub.com

ISBN: 978-1-63246-131-5

PRINTED IN THE UNITED STATES OF AMERICA

FIRST EDITION | FIRST PRINTING

Literary experience heals the wound, without undermining the privilege, of individuality.

—C. S. Lewis, *An Experiment in Criticism*

PINNED BY SENTENCES

WHEN I FELT AS IF I were coming apart in college, which was much of the time, I turned to George Eliot. Sometimes to Jane Austen or Henry James or Tolstoy—but mostly to Eliot, and above all to her masterpiece, *Middlemarch*. Why would an 1872 novel about the English provinces feel like salvation to an urban American child of the 1960s and '70s? *Middlemarch*, to oversimplify, is the story of three marriages and three tangled inheritances, against the backdrop of English politics and medical practice in the 1830s. In 1983, I was a twenty-year-old who was struggling with an eating disorder, anxiety, and a tendency to screw up my romantic relationships. What could reading *Middlemarch* possibly do about these difficulties?

It was a summer roommate who introduced me to the book. I met Caroline in an Introduction to German class at Yale. She was sweet and quiet with beautiful eyes hidden by large glasses, a young woman who in her self-possession seemed closer to thirty than to my age. She had a longtime boyfriend, a graduate student who was practically the only person she spent time with, and together they were as sensible and unexcitable as a long-married couple. When Caroline wasn't with her boyfriend, she read. She read voluminously. Among the many books she consumed that summer was *Middlemarch*. She was reading it for the second time—she claimed its 900-some pages flew by. I was intrigued and bought my own copy, a fat Penguin edition. On its cover, a young woman in a dark tunic and white skirt, her bonnet thrown back, walked along a fence overlooking yellow fields.

The reason I stayed in town over the summers was that my psychoanalyst was there. At fifty-seven, I must be among the youngest living graduates of classic psychoanalytic psychotherapy. For six years, three times a week (and sometimes more often), I walked down to the Yale Child Study Center, lay down on a couch, and free-associated. In those days analysis was the psychotherapy of choice for educated, affluent American sufferers from life. My father had been "shrunk," and my mother too; when I started showing signs of distress, this was the option they turned to.

In the years soon after, insurance companies stopped wanting to pay for such intensive, long-term therapy, and at the same time the field of psychology turned against Freudian theory, the basis for psychoanalysis, as being empirically unverifiable. Psychoanalysis is much maligned these days, but it was probably perfect for me. I was ruminative, desperate to sort myself out, and didn't like people telling me what to do. What could be better than a form of therapy that involved me getting to say anything and the analyst almost nothing?

In addition, the language of desire and shame, and the belief in hidden psychological wellsprings of behavior, came naturally to me. I took to analysis for the same reasons I'd taken to reading novels as a child: both were about the circumstances we grow up in and what we do with them, about human character and the outcomes it creates. I also took to analysis for the same reason I took to *writing* fiction: the free association method, in which the patient says whatever comes into her mind, no matter how absurd, irrelevant, or fragmentary, was like the initial stages of composing a short story. What goes down on the page is dreamlike and malleable, before the writer has to start figuring out what the story is and how she will stitch it together.

I was introverted at twenty, uneasy around noisy college

pursuits that involved crowds and boisterous drinking. I didn't care about football games and didn't thrill to the a cappella group performances that were a hallowed social ritual at Yale. Mostly I went to classes and my analytic sessions, did my schoolwork, hung out with my boyfriend (or wished I had one), and read. I liked to read in and of itself and because I felt safe when I did; it was a way to have all kinds of experiences without going anywhere and without getting hurt, physically or emotionally. There was no particular trauma in my upbringing to account for my skittish and escapist temperament. It was, simply, my temperament. My classes as a literature major were heavy on theory: deconstruction, psychoanalytic theory, feminist theory. There was surprisingly little novel reading. So I worked my way through this part of the Western canon on my own, in the lovely, quiet, postmidnight hours before sleep, after my classwork was done. The writers who captivated me shared a certain aspect of voice, a stance toward their subject matter. This voice had authority. It was possessed of a remarkable amount of knowledge about the world and offered its views assertively. "Pierre was one of those people who are strong only when they feel themselves perfectly pure," writes Tolstoy in *War and Peace*. "Miss Brooke had that kind of beauty which seems to be thrown into relief by poor dress," begins *Middlemarch*.

For a confused young adult eager to grab on to any certainties about life, this voice was extremely appealing. The narrators of the novels I read stood on secure ground, confident of their take on any situation. If a genie had appeared at the time and granted me one wish, and if I'd been self-aware enough to articulate it, I would have answered: "Give me a vantage point from which I can see what is true and good." Henry James, Jane Austen, George Eliot, Leo Tolstoy, Edith Wharton, E. M. Forster—or, at least, the narrators who were their stand-ins—all had that vantage point. I enjoyed other authorial styles too: Faulkner's hypnotic intricacies, the operatic emotionalism of Dostoevsky, the linguistic high spirits of Bellow. But I clung to the sentences of the Apollonian masters. Those sentences might be complicated, but they parsed perfectly. They were clear, analytical, witty, and wise.

On my worst days, when I felt like a skin that could barely contain the misery inside, it was literally sentence by sentence that I got through the minutes and hours. Opening *Pride and Prejudice* or *The Mill on the Floss*, I channeled my attention down the clauses and subclauses. It took patience to read those longish, well-balanced sentences, and I needed that slowing down. I absorbed one unit of meaning, then the next. What meditators do with breath, I did with sentences. They gave my frightened, obsession-prone brain something to do, my exorbitant feelings a focus. They kept me in one place, focused and calm, or at least calm enough.

George Eliot's *Middlemarch* held me most of all.

Eliot, born Mary Ann—sometimes Mary Anne or Marian—Evans in 1819, was a prominent translator and critic of her time, much of whose early work appeared in the influential *Westminster Review*, of which she eventually became the unacknowledged editor. (John Chapman, the titular editor, got the credit.) If that were all, only academics would know of her today. But when she was in her late thirties, her companion, George Henry Lewes, encouraged her to start writing fiction. He suspected before she did that her highly observant and empathic nature would lend itself to the construction of stories about imaginary human beings. In her journals Eliot later wrote that she had always wanted to try her hand at fiction but suspected she wouldn't be good at dialogue or scene—anything, really, but description. Lewes nagged her until she finally began.

Often enough, intellectuals who turn to fiction find it

hard to create immediacy; rather than inhabit characters, they move them around as idea-pieces. Eliot, it turned out, did not have this problem. Her earliest attempts, the three novellas that later made up her first book, *Scenes of Clerical Life*, came into being vibrant and fully fledged. At first, fearing that her work would not be taken seriously, she published under a man's name—"George" was an homage to Lewes—and few suspected that *Scenes* and the novel that followed, *Adam Bede*, were by a woman (Charles Dickens, who wrote to Eliot early on to express his admiration and his hunch, was a notable exception). She was not outed for several years, by which time she was a popular and critical sensation and the truth could no longer damage her.

In 2013 the cultural magazine *n+1* ran a wonderfully wonky article by the Stanford Literary Lab that analyzed sentence structure in well-known novels from the late eighteenth through the early twentieth centuries.[1] *Middlemarch's* opening line ("Miss Brooke had that kind of beauty which seems to be thrown into relief by poor dress") got dedicated attention. The article's authors noted that while the first part of the sentence is narrative—"Miss Brooke had . . . beauty"—the second is commentary, an attempt to categorize and draw implications. In other words, from the first sentence on, Eliot merges storytelling and the essay. After novels, I adore the essay form the most: the imprint of an individual voice combined with an analytical impulse directed inward or outward or both. It should be no surprise that my favorite author is one who blends fiction and the essay so seamlessly. Eliot delights in digressions on science, medicine, politics, fashion, manners, and, not least, human nature, digressions that really aren't ones in the end, as they deepen our understanding of her characters and their situations. From the first she was set apart for me by her ability to move from a young woman's disappointment in her new husband to a comment about how hard it is for us to see that other people have "an equivalent center of self" to our own, from a description of men drinking in a pub to an observation about the natural conservatism of farmers. Eliot wrote sentences that kept my brain busy following suggestions, connections, conclusions. They were lessons in how to think.

And there was something more. Eliot was interested in complicated questions of how we treat one another, questions of kindness and cruelty. So was I, a bent from earliest childhood, when I liked to make up lists of everything good and bad I'd done that day. (Good: let my younger brother choose the TV channel. Bad: hit my brother.) James and Tolstoy and Wharton all have a narrative authority similar to Eliot's, but are emotionally a couple of shades colder. Maybe they are just more resigned to the amount of pain people visit upon each other. C. S. Lewis wrote of reading Tolstoy's *War and Peace* that he "felt everywhere . . . that sublime indifference to the life or death, success or failure, of the chief characters, which is not a blank indifference at all, but almost like submission to the will of God."[2] Eliot is not so willing to submit—tenderhearted, she aligns herself with human beings, not God. She always feels the pain and always implies that we can find ways to ameliorate it. What she is really always writing about is love, love in the broadest sense, and how we might become more capable of it.

Eliot never specifies the exact location of Middlemarch, the town that gives her novel its title, but we might imagine it as Coventry, where Mary Ann Evans spent her twenties, and which is more or less in the middle of the country. ("March" is an archaic English word for a tract of land.) "Middlemarch" is also meant to convey averageness, everydayness: an American rendition of the name would be Middletown, and an allegorical one would be Everytown.

The two most prominent characters in this Everytown are Dorothea Brooke, a nineteen-year-old orphan with a comfortable inheritance, and Tertius Lydgate, a twenty-seven-year-old London-educated doctor interested in bringing progressive reforms to medical practice and research. If this latter plotline sounds dull, remember that typical treatments of the time involved bloodletting and the ingestion of dubious drugs that doctors were incentivized to prescribe because they earned money on their sale. Autopsies were uncommon and the knowledge of human anatomy limited. Lydgate refuses to sell drugs, and he is interested, to the horror of the community, in doing postmortems. He wants to bring medicine out of medieval superstition and into the age of science. He has ambitions to make discoveries through his study of human tissues.

You could call Dorothea and Lydgate *Middlemarch*'s protagonists, but really the protagonist of the novel is the whole town. The breadth of the portrait—the attention paid to everyone from the landed gentry through the new industrial middle class, the traditional artisan and farming classes, all the way down to the horse traders, housemaids, and itinerant drunks— filled me, upon first reading, with delight in the exuberant variety of mid-nineteenth-century

English life. Some novels, some really excellent novels, are like fascinating but small and sealed-off rooms; *Middlemarch* made me feel that I was out in the open country under a great blue sky, pulling big breaths of fresh air into my lungs.

I had crushes on both Dorothea and Lydgate. I identified more with Lydgate, given his intellectual passion. He is handsome, very intelligent, graceful in an utterly masculine way, and gentle; in addition to wanting to be him I wanted to marry him. (Unfortunately for him and for me, he marries the town belle, Rosamond Vincy.) Dorothea has been educated to the standard of a proper Englishwoman in the time of George IV—which is to say, not very well. She is religious, emotional, and eager to devote her life to some worthy cause. When the novel opens, she is busy drawing up plans in the hopes of convincing her guardian uncle to improve the tenant-farmer cottages on his estate. Soon enough she marries a man more than twice her age, Edward Casaubon, with the idea that she will enable him to finish his long-in-the-making scholarly study on religious mythology. (It will turn out that Casaubon is incapable of finishing it—has indeed barely put pen to paper.) If I wanted to be Lydgate, I thought I *should* be Dorothea. She has her author's empathic qualities, and, like Lydgate, she is determined to be a force for good in the world. *Middlemarch* has a lot to say about what actually does do good in the world—but I'll get to that later.

What both Dorothea and Lydgate end up confronting is a gap between their aspirations and their everyday reality. That sort of gap was of great interest to me at twenty, nearly Dorothea's age exactly. I'd wanted to be a writer since I was nine or ten years old but—particularly after getting only a B+ in Yale's famous writing course, Daily Themes—was beginning to suspect that maybe I wasn't the talent I had once imagined. At times I pictured myself as some sort of intellectual, but the truth was I was too dreamy and easily bored for sustained abstract thought. I also wanted to be a good person and wasn't at all sure that I was one. I didn't actually, like Dorothea, love helping people. If you were looking for the friend who would help you move your boxes from one dorm room to another, or type a paper for you, it wasn't me.

One night, I went out to a bar with a charming friend-slash-boyfriend (I had a number of those during college) after we'd seen the movie *Amadeus* together. *Amadeus*, you may remember, is the story of Wolfgang Amadeus Mozart, as narrated by his rival Antonio Salieri. Salieri, a successful court musician and actual historical figure, is depicted—unfairly, many have argued—as a worker bee, someone whose compositions are leaden and willed, while Mozart is a genius, a conduit for heavenly harmonies who arranges notes as easily as he breathes. Salieri is embittered: Why does everything come so easily to the other man? Why, no matter how he tries, can he not make music as transcendent as Mozart's?

My friend-slash-boyfriend wrote poetry and drew, and over our beers we admitted to each other that already we felt like Salieris, not Mozarts. We were young, but we knew enough to know we weren't spectacularly gifted. We would be plodders, not angels. "To mediocrity!" Jeff cried, raising his bottle. "To mediocrity!" I agreed, raising mine.

But of course we hoped that we were wrong.

In *Middlemarch*, then, I found a detailed, compassionate exploration of what happens when, bit by bit, life encroaches on a person's fantasies of fulfillment, whether those fantasies have to do with artistic success or saintliness or intellectual insight or wealth or love. Can that person adjust? If she does, does that mean she's betrayed her highest self? Or is there something better, more lasting, on the other side of an ideal? And what about my ideal, which was *to write just like George*

Eliot? Was that an ideal with any speck of reality in it?

Years passed. I read *Middlemarch* again about a decade later, when I was living in New York City with my husband and still clinging to the notion that someday I would be able to write like George Eliot. Not as well as her, of course, but *like* her. I read *Middlemarch* again in my forties as the mother of young children. And I have just read it again to write this volume. This last time I was experiencing crises that were as intense as, though very different from, the ones I experienced at twenty. One of my children was suffering from debilitating anxiety and depression. We were three years into the Trump presidency, with its disrespect for the rule of law, its coarsening of public discourse, its purposeful intimidation of everyone from immigrants to public servants trying to do their job of upholding the Constitution. Trump continued to be enthusiastically supported by nearly half of all Americans, which meant that even if he could be ousted in the next election, we were going to be living with Trumpism for a long time. And the coronavirus had just landed on America's shores. I began to write the pages you are now reading as social distancing became a mantra and most of the retail and cultural spaces in my area were shuttered. My grown children had returned home, and our family was leaving the house only for the occasional walk around the neighborhood. Once again I found that George Eliot's sentences pinned me to sanity.

As people all over America were instructed to self-quarantine, the author Yiyun Li launched a virtual book group to work its way through *War and Peace* during this time of isolation. On the blog of the magazine *A Public Space*, she posted comments about each day's twelve-to-fifteen-page reading. Early on, she quoted the Viennese writer Stefan Zweig on Tolstoy: "When Tolstoy is telling a tale, we do not hear his breathing. He tells it as upland peasants climb their native hills; slowly, equably, step by step; without rushes, without impatience, without fatigue, without weakness; and the throbbing of his heart never troubles the smooth tone of his voice. That is why we do not lose our composure when we are in his company."

And that is why *Middlemarch* rescued me as an undergraduate, and all over again in 2020. It bestows upon its readers composure. In these last many months, when I often felt swamped by fear and grief, I experienced once again the deep comfort of sentences. Sentences that pierced through the noise of existence and laid bare its true operations. Sentences that twisted and turned, elongated and contracted, in order to assemble a universe in which people as real to me as the ones I know personally strive and celebrate and mourn. Some of them find happiness, some failure; all suffer. All of them have the gift of free will and opportunities to make choices that will matter. I hear Eliot's authority in the prose of a handful of contemporary writers, among them Edith Pearlman and Edward P. Jones. Their narrators, like Eliot's, make life make sense to me. Their breadth and clarity give me a greater sense of possibility and therefore hope. When I am troubled, I know that, like Eliot, they will remind me that human beings are marvelous and sacred creatures, and that goodness finds its way through the cracks of our trivial, wrongheaded, misfortune-struck world.

FUNNY GIRL

GEORGE ELIOT DOES NOT HAVE a reputation for being funny.

Certainly, Eliot did not write novels primarily to entertain. She had serious intentions, as well as some quarrels with the popular fiction of her day, which she expressed in her *Westminster Review* article "Silly Novels by Lady Novelists." Contemporary personal accounts of Eliot suggest that she was earnest and grave, rather like Dorothea Brooke. Especially late in her life, when she was extremely famous, she was described by visitors as sibyl-like, a priestess with a low, quiet voice who rarely smiled. That version of George Eliot, combined with the impression she gives in her novels of great learning, has come down to us and scared some into thinking that her novels are humorless, dutiful slogs. In addition, after her death, the "interfering" narrator—who breaks in, as Eliot's often does, to make pronouncements about human nature and the ways of the world—began to fall out of fashion. Eliot, as perhaps its greatest exponent, was now seen as didactic and tedious.[3]

But her novels are, in fact, funny. Some of the humor comes from Eliot's terrific ear for speech: she neatly skewers the gossips, humbugs, bloviators, hypochondriacs, and cranks who exist in every society. I can't think of another novel with as broad an array of speech patterns; each of its many characters has one as distinct as a fingerprint. Eliot's minor characters can be grasped whole simply from a few lines of dialogue. In this way, she reminds me of Dickens. But most of Eliot's humor is slyer than caricature, wittier. The wit is in how she draws our attention to the innumerable ways in which we human beings misread ourselves and the world around us. Eliot is generous about our fallibility, which usually stems from our vanity. The fun comes from her amused and indulgent way of describing the great muddle we make of things.

My enthusiasm for *Middlemarch* was first cemented by a line just a couple of pages in. We are told of Dorothea's beauty and her love of fresh air and the outdoors, which strike the townspeople as being at odds with her deep religiosity. (Our first hint that Dorothea will be a character of contradictions.) Men find her quite attractive, especially when she is out horseback riding, which she loves. Eliot continues: "Riding was an indulgence which she allowed herself in spite of conscientious qualms; she felt that she enjoyed it in a pagan sensuous way, and always looked forward to renouncing it."

How refreshing! I could see right away that the story of this would-be saint was not going to be told straight, that the narrator would not try to force me to take Dorothea as seriously as she takes herself. I smiled as I recognized my own tendency to alternate between the pleasure of eating favorite foods and the pleasure of refusing them. As a nine- or ten-year-old, I'd held on to my Halloween candy for months, parceling it out with excruciating slowness, getting terrific satisfaction from the fact that I still had a stash long after my brother had decimated his own. (Had I still been keeping my good/bad tallies, I might have documented this as: Good: didn't eat my candy all at once. Bad: lorded it over my brother.) In my case, there was no thought of renouncing candy altogether, but Eliot nailed the way in which giving up or postponing pleasure can become a different, and smugger, type of satisfaction.

I was going to like this narrator.

Dorothea is being courted by her neighbor Sir James Chettam, who will later marry her younger sister. So uninteresting does she consider Sir James that she doesn't even realize he's pursuing her. One day he brings Dorothea a white Maltese puppy because he's noticed they are a fad among fashionable ladies. Dorothea, never fashionable, tells Sir James that she doesn't like animals bred to be pets: she prefers those in the wild, who strike her as having "souls something like our own." At this reply, Sir James hands the dog to his servant, who seems likely enough to have it killed—a fate that Dorothea, wrapped up in her lecture, apparently hasn't considered. Particularly in the early sections of the book, Dorothea's determination to be helpful to others is made to seem funny. Nobody wants or needs her help all that much, and she sometimes finds herself wishing that the people around her were suffering more, so she could do something about it.

Eliot's humor often has to do with the foible of self-importance. At one point, Lydgate's wife observes that he has "relapsed into what she inwardly called his moodiness—a name which to her covered his thoughtful preoccupation with other subjects than herself." The puffed-up, smooth-talking auctioneer Mr. Borthrop Trumbull "would have liked to have the universe under his hammer, feeling that it would go at a higher figure for his recommendation."

In one of the most famous passages of *Middlemarch*, Eliot tells us that if you place a lighted candle against a mirror with scratches on it, "the scratches will seem to arrange themselves in a fine series of concentric circles round that little sun. It is demonstrable that the scratches are going everywhere impartially, and it is only your candle which produces the flattering illusion of a concentric arrangement." This, she says, is a parable. Each of us is a candle, a consciousness, that sees in the random data of the universe—what people do, what they say to us, the weather—a pattern with our individual self at the center. Over and over, Eliot shows us the discrepancy between the arbitrariness of the scratches and our insistent patternmaking, and coaxes us to laugh— at ourselves as well as her characters. Every time I do laugh, it's like releasing air from the painfully inflated version of self that I'm condemned to wear like a bulky costume.

Dorothea's sister, Celia, is in every way the conventional creature that Dorothea, with her solemnity and social-improvement schemes, is not. Whatever "everybody" thinks is what Celia thinks; it was what she already thought before she consulted anyone. She knows instantly what to approve or disapprove of and is utterly at home with herself, lacking any nagging feeling that she should be better or different. The remarkable thing is that, as a novelist, Eliot is as fond of Celia as she is of Dorothea.

Once again, it all comes back to Eliot's stance. She clearly thinks Dorothea is more *interesting* than her sister—that's why the novel is about her, not Celia. But she doesn't necessarily think Dorothea is worthier or more lovable. Eliot has plenty of respect for those who fit in, who make society run smoothly because they don't quarrel with its suppositions or its rules. Celia and Sir James Chettam are such people. They are decent, honorable, trustworthy, and narrow-minded. Eliot doesn't despise them for their narrow-mindedness (which at its worst shades into xenophobia and anti-Semitism) any more than she despises Dorothea for her excessive moralism. Or any more than she despises her shady horse dealers for being shady or her careless young gentlemen for being careless, even when that carelessness hurts others. She recognizes the hard-won canniness of those horse dealers and the vigorous optimism of careless young gentlemen. Perhaps because she wasn't one herself, she likes easygoing people: Chettam, and also the Reverend Farebrother and Mr. Cadwallader, whom we will meet later.

She likes spiritedness and vitality of any kind; and for her characters who are inhibited and weak, she feels pity, not scorn.

Another significant category of Eliot's humor deals with ignorance, which is perhaps just a subset of vanity. Mrs. Dollop is a very minor character in the novel, the landlady of a pub frequented by local tradespeople. It's a precinct into which the main characters, who come from or have found their way into the higher classes, do not stray. The denizens of the Tankard—shoemakers and dyers, barbers and glaziers— are not stupid, but they are also not very good at separating rumor from fact. When a scandal arises in Middlemarch around Nicholas Bulstrode, a prominent banker, some at the pub float sordid conjectures about Bulstrode's past. The more they talk, the more they believe their own inventions. Mrs. Dollop is one of these, and "had often to resist the shallow pragmatism of customers disposed to think that their reports from the outer world were of equal force with what had 'come up' in her mind." (It's probably unnecessary to draw the parallels with the creators and spreaders of fake news today.)

Eliot in no way singles out the lower middle classes as

more likely to display ignorance. Mr. Brooke, Dorothea's uncle and guardian, has money and influence and is a local magistrate: that is, a lay judge before whom less serious criminal cases are brought. He's the sort of person who has "looked into" every subject of study and retained little of it, who name-drops famous thinkers and politicians he has met and learned nothing from; his mind is a cluttered, disorganized wardrobe of odds and ends. He is well meaning, without any fixed beliefs, and utterly ineffectual. When he decides to run for Parliament, he enthusiastically instructs his aide to write a speech containing "not ideas, you know, but a way of putting them." (As a vote approaches, he also has the impression that "waverers were likely to be allured by wavering statements.")

Lydgate, a much more formidable individual, is genuinely at home in the world of ideas but remains clueless about his inner nature. He has, says Eliot, "a confidence in his own powers and integrity much fortified by contempt for petty obstacles or seductions of which he had had no experience." That experience, one suspects, will be soon to arrive.

For me, reading *Middlemarch* is like drinking a carbonated beverage that sends bubbles up my chest and prickling into my nose; my body idles on a low chuckle. Eliot is not about the big occasional guffaw but the constant tickling of a mirthful outlook on life. Though we can laugh at Mrs. Dollop—I feel, as with every character in *Middlemarch*, that I have met her at some point in my life—there is a quality of embrace in Eliot's attitude toward her. Mrs. Dollop is entertaining and assertive. She's a businesswoman who holds her own in a world of men. We later learn, in passing, that all her children have died. She is *real*. So is Mr. Brooke, who is touchingly kindhearted when it comes to Dorothea and Celia, unable to be the dictatorial parental substitute his neighbors think he should be. (Most significantly, he will not forbid Dorothea from choosing Edward Casaubon as a spouse when the community believes she is making a terrible mistake. Which she is.)

There is remarkably little cruelty in Eliot's imaginative world; she seems to feel that unmixed cruelty is an aberration. Our unkindest acts are usually instead the result of fear and misunderstanding. The two possible exceptions in *Middlemarch* are the elderly, dying Peter Featherstone and John Raffles, a con man and drunk. Featherstone entertains himself by dangling the possibility of an inheritance in front of now one relative, now another, taking pleasure in watching his extended family grovel and fight with one another. At times we glimpse the loneliness and unhappiness beneath the mean-spirited games. He has no wife, no family life. He is an old man who has lost or never had the ability to love. In its place is only the gratification of exerting control over others. I feel sorry for him, even though he is a destructive figure.

Raffles is a different matter, a two-dimensional being who exists primarily to enable certain plot developments. Here, uncharacteristically, Eliot forgets that every flame of consciousness believes itself at the center of life's pattern. We never get inside Raffles's mind or learn why he does the things he does. He dies a protracted, terrorized death, and I can't help but feel a little sorry for him too. So potently does Eliot create her general atmosphere of compassion that it softens my reading even of characters toward whom she is less generous.

Once I'd read George Eliot, it became impossible to write a nasty or unethical character into my own fiction without second thoughts. Her characterizations were the gold standard to which I aspired, and I always sought to understand the way "the other" (anyone not a point-of-view character) might be thinking or feeling in a given scene. This led me into some difficulties. The editor of my first novel,

The Understory, complained that I was overelaborating a quite minor (nasty, unethical) character—the protagonist's landlord—and patiently reminded me of E. M. Forster's famous distinction between flat and round characters. Flat characters, otherwise known as types, are defined by one basic characteristic or motivation, which never changes. They can be summed up in a single sentence; my landlord's would have been, "I will do anything to evict my tenant." A round character is unpredictable and complex. Only round characters can be tragic, Forster says, and flat characters are "best when they are comic." I'd read *Aspects of the Novel* more than once, but I'd still somehow taken away from it that flat characters were failures of authorial talent or effort. Forster says no such thing; he even comments that "in Russian novels, where they [flat characters] so seldom occur, they would be a decided help." My *Understory* editor felt that my minor character needed to be flat so that he didn't steal energy from the scenes he was in. This was absolutely correct, and I toned the landlord down, to the benefit of my narrative. Sometimes villains have to be allowed to be villains . . . even if George Eliot very rarely stooped to that.

For many years, I've meditated regularly, using the method

of focusing on my breath. My meditation app advises that when, inevitably, I lose that focus, I simply note the thought or feeling that distracted me, before returning my attention. The instructor uses the comparison of spotting an unusual bird sitting on a branch a few feet away, a colorful bird one has never seen before. One would likely respond by being pleasantly intrigued. Likewise, in becoming aware of a thought while meditating, one might respond with "curiosity and wonder": "How interesting: that's anger"; "How interesting: that's envy." The approach is meant to circumvent our tendency to berate ourselves when we drop focus, or to see certain thoughts or feelings as bad. They're not bad; they're just there.

George Eliot's stance toward her characters is like the meditator's stance toward thought: full of curiosity and wonder. The result is a tone of tolerance, humility, generosity—and humor. One of the most significant things I learned as a young writer was that what happens in a story is far less important than how the narrator tells that story. The narrator *is* the story. She is a way of looking at the world, a lens through which the reader sees everything. The narrator embodies the values of her constructed world, which come through via her tone, diction, and rhythm; when and where she employs comedy; and what she chooses to look at or ignore. That Eliot finds human beings amusing, absurd, and lovable *is* her story: of *Middlemarch* as well as of other works such as *Scenes of Clerical Life* and *The Mill on the Floss*. That she speaks to the reader as if the reader, too, takes this view has the result of prying open the reader's heart, increasing her compassion, clearing her vision. That clarity is medicine. When I read Eliot, I am somehow better, more humble, more generous, more understanding—and I find life more funny.

MICROCOSM

MIDDLEMARCH TAKES PLACE IN THE early 1830s, as the massive dislocations of industrialization were swelling the cities of Europe, creating a large population of urban poor and a much smaller class of urban nouveau riche. The novel doesn't deal with either of those demographics, but it otherwise accounts for almost every type of human being you can find in a town of any size. There are those who are comfortable and idle; those who sweat to earn a living; servants, employers of servants, and independent workers; those whose livelihood relies on flattering and pleasing other people and those who needn't worry about such things. There are strict parents and indulgent ones, naughty children and rule followers, restless natures and homebodies, the highly disciplined and the lazy. There are those who have an elastic definition of the truth and those who can't bear telling a lie, those who vote in elections for change and those who fight to keep things the same. There are the educated, the uneducated, meddlers and avoiders and complainers, those who speak from the heart and those who can't get out of their heads, those quick to judge and those quick to forgive. I could go on.

Middlemarch somehow includes everybody. At least, that's how it feels to me. Even a novel like *War and Peace* can look narrow beside it, dealing as it primarily does with the Russian aristocracy and the military.

Eliot doesn't construct this busy world just to show us she can; she does so because community is at the heart of her interests as a writer. In a letter to her publisher, John Blackwood, Eliot explained that her aim in *Middlemarch* was to illustrate "the gradual action of ordinary causes rather than exceptional." Many novels make use of a dramatic event—a war, an epidemic, political upheaval—in order to explore how it shapes human behavior. Eliot works in the opposite direction. She wants to show us how human behavior *creates* our world, how the things we do every day forge chains of results that have a powerful impact on others. In turn, we are shaped by the small actions of those we may hardly even know.

Americans have a novelistic tradition of the outsider protagonist: Huck Finn, Jay Gatsby, Bigger Thomas, Tom Ripley, Dean Moriarty. These are men (almost always they are men) who attempt to extricate themselves from the society that has formed them and reinvent themselves, often outside of the law. Eliot's protagonists, in contrast, by and large accept that they live within a dense network of interdependencies. Her outsiders are never all that outside. Dorothea Brooke is seen as eccentric by her neighbors, but they claim her all the same, and she feels responsible toward them. She has no thought of renouncing ties and blazing her own solitary, much less criminal, path in the world. And this is not just because she is a woman. The men in the novel, too, find themselves knit into the social fabric, whether they want to be or not. Tertius Lydgate comes from elsewhere and believes he can remain above petty Middlemarch professional intriguing, but discovers this to be impossible, particularly after he marries into a local family. Will Ladislaw, a nephew of Dorothea's scholar husband, also comes to Middlemarch after being educated abroad. He fancies himself a sort of Percy Bysshe Shelley, a poet and Romantic, but becomes ensnared in a grubby local scandal not of his own making. One of Eliot's firmest beliefs is that in ways good and bad, we never stand alone in the world. We are not, with apologies to "Invictus," the captains of our souls and the masters of our fates. This doesn't mean we are helpless; far from it. It simply means that other people, individually and in groups, exert a significant influence over our lives, even when we pride ourselves on being fierce individualists.

Eliot didn't lament this. She was not a radical by nature, even as in many ways she lived a radical life: supporting herself with her writing at a time when this was exceedingly rare for a woman, setting up household with George Henry Lewes despite the fact that he was legally married to someone else. (His wife had a child by another man, and because Lewes knowingly accepted the child as his own, he was unable to divorce her later, when she went on to have more out-of-wedlock children. Eliot considered herself to be married to Lewes and went by the name Marian Evans Lewes.) Eliot was well aware of the ways in which traditional societies muffled or persecuted people who were different. Her father threatened to throw her out of the house when, as a young woman, she began to question her religious faith. When her brother learned of her relationship with Lewes, he did not speak to her for twenty-two years, and many other people, because of Lewes, would not visit or be seen with her. But Eliot also saw the beauty in convention, which binds people together and stabilizes existence. The England Eliot describes in *Middlemarch* is neither rigidly fixed in tradition nor dramatically in flux. Changes are arriving, slowly: the railways are being built; political reform is expanding the number of English citizens entitled to vote. Eliot's characters, like people in all eras, straddle the old and the new. But from the perspective of the twenty-first century, the world of *Middlemarch* is a stately, predictable one. Most people live out their lives near their families; everyday objects are made by local artisans and not at some faraway factory; the working day is still marked out by the rising and setting of the sun. The country is at peace.

This stability and familiarity allow for a great deal of social tolerance. Mr. Cadwallader is the rector (parish priest) of Tipton, where the Brookes live; he is a genial sort, more interested in fishing than in writing sermons or saving souls. His wife, Elinor, is an older version of Celia, with a sharper tongue; her opinion represents the "sensible" opinion of the Middlemarch upper classes. Mrs. Cadwallader is a snob, a cheapskate, intelligent, and often quite kind. Like her neighbors, she sees that Dorothea's intended, Edward Casaubon, is a pretentious and dreary man, someone who has no business marrying a passionate nineteen-year-old. Mrs. C and Sir James Chettam, Dorothea's ex-suitor (who still feels a great deal of protectiveness toward her), together ask Mr. Cadwallader to convince Mr. Brooke to forbid the marriage. Mr. C responds that one can never get Mr. Brooke to commit to anything: "Brooke is a very good fellow, but pulpy; he will run into any mold, but he won't keep shape." When pressed, he then argues that he can't see any truly valid objections to Casaubon: he (Cadwallader) doesn't care about Mr. Casaubon's dusty studies, but then Mr. Casaubon doesn't care about Mr. Cadwallader's fishing tackle. "He has always been civil to me," Mr. C concludes, and anyway who is to say what will make a girl like Dorothea happy? (To this, Mrs. Cadwallader replies fancifully that somebody once put a drop of Mr. Casaubon's blood under a magnifying glass and found that "it was all semicolons and parentheses.")

Middlemarchers see each other's flaws and oddities, but they mostly let each other be. At another point, we see Mrs. Cadwallader in a conversation with the lower-class Mrs. Fitchett, the lodge keeper at Tipton. Mrs. C, interested in buying some fowl from Mrs. Fitchett, offers her too little money for them, arguing that Mrs. Fitchett has been "half paid" already with Mr. Cadwallader's weekly sermons. After

Mrs. Cadwallader drives off, Mrs. Fitchett can do nothing but laugh over the other woman's relentless stinginess, and we're told that the local farmers and laborers "would have felt a sad lack of conversation but for the stories about what Mrs. Cadwallader said and did." "A much more exemplary character," writes Eliot, ". . . would have been less socially uniting."

Mrs. Cadwallader is one of three characters threaded through *Middlemarch* who act as social mouthpieces, letting us glimpse general opinion on matters pertaining to the main characters. All are gossips or information spreaders who bind together members of their set. Mrs. Cadwallader shows us what the well born think; Mr. Hawley, a lawyer and the town clerk, represents the middle classes; and Mrs. Dollop the lower ones. All three, whatever their personal shortcomings, possess a great degree of common sense, and they tend to be rather right even when they are wrong. It would have been harsh and presumptuous for the Cadwalladers to interfere in Dorothea's marriage—but Mrs. C is correct about Casaubon, who proves a disaster as a husband. Mr. Hawley has a temper, but his reasoning is usually sound. And while Mrs. Dollop, as we've seen, is partial to alternative facts, she and her customers are onto something about Mr. Bulstrode, who indeed is not the paragon of virtue he pretends to be.

Then again, at every level of social class, outsiders like Bulstrode (or Lydgate or Will Ladislaw) are scrutinized by Middlemarchers in a way that long-familiar families and neighbors simply are not. Outsiders do in fact pose a threat. Lydgate's new, more empirically based ways of practicing medicine challenge the credibility and livelihoods of the town's established doctors. Bulstrode wields power over those who are in debt to him. Ladislaw is a freethinker who might give other people the wrong ideas about obedience to authority and the proper work for a gentleman. All three disturb the townspeople's complacency and security and are seen as arrogant in their refusal to play by Middlemarch rules.

We Americans have a lot of experience being outsiders. We move a lot. Many of us leave home for our schooling or take jobs that send us to a new location every few years. We sometimes move elsewhere simply because we can. As a result, we more often choose than inherit our communities. Arriving in a new town, we find the house of worship in which we feel most at home, track down the local crafts circle or theater group or service organization. We suss out the vibe and hope to be accepted, to fit in. Some of us (I include myself here) are not talented joiners and may take a long time to feel part of any community. I have childhood memories of how, on the first day of summer camp each year, the counselors would make us sit in a circle and play a game "to get to know each other." This friendly ice-breaking tradition practically made me hyperventilate with discomfort. I wanted to get to know the other kids one-on-one, if at all. The older I get, the more relaxed I've become in groups, the more I have come to genuinely enjoy them (up to a point). But my gist is that in a place like Middlemarch, you don't have to seek out community; you are simply part of one. In current-day America, community is something you have to *do*.

The lack of an inherited community and tradition seems to me a sizable disadvantage for a writer. I am the descendant of European Jews, most of them likely poor, who came to America around the turn of the twentieth century. Their lives in Poland and Russia and Lithuania must have been difficult, because they didn't talk about them—or if they did, their children, my grandparents, didn't pass those stories on. That first generation to be born in the States was very preoccupied with "being American," whatever that meant to them. They were legally citizens, but as Jews they knew they would always appear as outsiders to some. This may have stoked their fierce desire to claim America's rituals and habits as their own. They gave up most of the religious observances their parents had brought with them and dressed pointedly in the latest styles; they even celebrated Christmas, which they considered a secular national holiday. (For my husband and me, more secure in our Americanness and less secure in our Jewishness, celebrating Christmas would feel sacrilegious.)

In any case, I possess no old family stories and almost no photographs—I don't even know, for the most part, where exactly in Eastern Europe my family came from, although there is a German side of the family, more middle class, which kept better records. Once my forebears arrived in the US, they lived in cities: Chicago, New Haven, and Washington, DC. They were separated from the rhythms of the countryside, if they'd ever lived among those rhythms, and pursued the more atomized lives of urban people. Their children, the first generation born here, struggled up into the middle class, placing a great deal of importance on educating their own children, including my parents, who went to college and graduate school. My father became a lawyer, my mother a college professor. We too lived in the city. My childhood was rich in books and conversation but poor in engagement with the natural world. I didn't play in the yard; we had no yard. My outdoor activities were limited and structured: school recess, trips to the park with a housekeeper. I rarely saw animals. Any type of hands-on work seemed to take place at a distance, as my parents farmed out the cleaning to a maid and the fixing to the super. Neither of them knew how to paint a wall or sew a button or even cook much of anything. Fiction is built out of the concrete, and there was an odd lack of the concrete in my life. Or maybe I just wasn't that invested in what *was* there. I was bookish and my energies went largely into the imaginary: the *Wizard of Oz* series and E. B. White, Mary Poppins and Mrs. Piggle-Wiggle. The real world I gleaned through the fascinating 1911 *Encyclopedia Britannica* set my mother inherited from her father, which together with the 1972 *World Book* seemed to promise all the extant knowledge in the universe. Later, the feminist-inflected books my mother bought me (*Wonder Woman* comics and biographies of Queen Elizabeth I and Eleanor of Aquitaine) also made a huge impression. Books were delight and information, self-improvement and feeling, deep feeling. I cried over *Little Women* and *The Grapes of Wrath*. Maybe daily life just didn't measure up in intensity.

When my own kids were little, my husband and I sometimes read them a book that I bought for Father's Day one year because it was sweet and addressed the fact that young children often don't understand what a parent who works outside the house does all day. The book purported to show "all kinds of daddies at all kinds of jobs." (Today this book would probably be seen as too gender-specific to be published.) The next pages showed illustrations of daddies at those jobs. There were "daddies on fire trucks," "daddies digging holes," "tailor daddies and sailor daddies." My husband, like my father, is a lawyer. When we got to his page, it offered "lawyer daddies with egg-salad sandwiches in their briefcases." There was a picture of a man, a desk, and a sandwich. I thought this was hilarious, but my husband was depressed at the evidence that his job was so abstract, and therefore so uninteresting to a child, that an egg-salad sandwich was the most "fun" thing about it that the book could come up with.

As a matter of fact, one of the things I loved about my husband when I first met him was that he liked to do things with his hands. He fished and gardened. He could cut down small trees and solve plumbing and electrical problems. He was the kind of person who had built a radio from scratch when he was a kid. This ability to make and fix things was rooting to me, after a childhood spent, as it were, in the air, amid skyscrapers and ideas. My husband-to-be also came from an intact family, as I did not, my parents having split up when I was in my late teens. By the time I knew him, I dearly wanted to be more tied in to nature, to the tactile world, to a partner, to family. The communities depicted in *Middlemarch* are nothing if not tied in: to the past and tradition, to extended family, to neighbors, and to the neighbors' expectations. When I read the novel, I get to experience these kinds of bonds—their comfort and oppressiveness both—myself.

Two characters in *Middlemarch* embody the rising individualism that leads directly to our own times: the Vincy children, Rosamond and Fred. Their father is a manufacturer, a member of the thriving new middle class. He's made enough money to educate both children with an eye to advancing them socially. Rosamond is sent to a finishing school to acquire the graces that will attract a wealthy suitor; Fred, her younger brother, is meant to go into the clergy. Rosamond and Fred have been raised to expect comfort and pleasure without troubling themselves too much about where the money for these will come from, but at the same time they lack the noblesse oblige of the old aristocracy. They are the capitalistic future. Rosamond is pretty, elegant, and steely in pursuit of her desires, a young woman who never has to raise her voice to get her way. She marries Lydgate, seeing in the new doctor in town a step up in status, but her social climbing and her insistence on being materially pampered destroy Lydgate's dreams of pursuing medical research, and leave their marriage an empty shell. Fred's self-absorption leads to laziness and failure at school, and serious problems for the father of Mary Garth, a young woman he loves, after Mr. Garth guarantees a debt Fred takes on.

I was a Vincy kid, you could say, encouraged to do what pleased me, not to think about money, and to expect that whatever I wished for in life would likely come about. This might sound like a wonderful way to grow up, if your childhood was different, but it can lead to its own sorrows, as Fred's and Rosamond's stories show. In young adulthood, I received some painful lessons to the effect that attending to one's own wishes first is not always good for friendships and love relationships. A small example: Upon arriving in my dorm room for the start of sophomore year in college, my new roommate asked if I wanted the bottom or top bunk bed. I was nervous in top bunks and said I'd like the bottom. Later she complained to someone that I'd selfishly grabbed my choice—apparently I had been supposed to say I didn't care one way or the other and then enter an elaborate social dance that would enable us to decide who really needed the bottom bunk more. The problem was, I had been raised to answer questions about my wishes straightforwardly, and to this day I think there are merits in that, especially for a woman. But I could have used more training in hearing the unspoken needs of others, especially when more was at stake than a bunk bed. To be honest, those needs scared me. I feared being trapped in relationships or duties I couldn't get out of, and tended to choose solitude over the messiness of interdependence. Other people were a lot of work; easier not to get involved in the first place. The Eliot scholar Joan Bennett has written that all of Eliot's fiction is about "the discovery of a mean point between complete self-repression and unchecked self-indulgence."[4] Fred Vincy eventually learns how to fruitfully repress himself—to discipline himself to hard work and meeting his obligations—through his love for Mary Garth. Rosamond never learns that the desires and requirements of others are as important as her own.

Dorothea, at the other extreme, inclined to self-sacrifice, comes to wonder whether self-suppression is always desirable or even possible. Her marriage turns out to be even worse than Mrs. Cadwallader and Sir James feared. Not only is Casaubon incapable of warmth, but Dorothea's presence triggers long-suppressed insecurities about his work. In asking him innocent questions about his research, Dorothea becomes the embodiment of all the people who have doubted or snubbed him; he is terrified of her inquisitiveness because it threatens to expose how outdated and incoherent he secretly suspects his project to be. The more she tries to become close to him by offering to help him with his work— organizing or transcribing his notes, translating texts—the more unkindly he pushes her away. Stunned, Dorothea discovers her previously unknown capacity for resentment. We know, and she knows, that a lifetime of solitude devoted to this cold, rejecting man is a terrible fate for a vibrant young woman. She is being buried alive. But her ethics and her upbringing tell her that she must accept her lot.

This is perhaps one of the hardest parts of *Middlemarch* for a contemporary reader to accept. I *don't* accept it, but my attitude makes sense only because of the times I live in. In 1830, you did not leave a husband because he made you feel lonely, depressed, and helpless. You were lucky if you could leave him because he beat or starved you. There is no other existence for Dorothea to step into, no way that she can remain part of her community if she separates from her husband. Since she has to stay, all she can do is find a way to keep her feelings from destroying her. She works to find empathy for her husband, visits her sister, continues to search out ways to help the less fortunate. Reading this section of the novel, I am gripped and horrified. Horrified because I am watching the unfolding of one of my greatest fears, that of being trapped and wholly dominated by another human being. Gripped because it gives me an image of what a dignified survival might look like under such circumstances. But while Dorothea's struggle to transcend her hurt and pain is heroic to me, it would eventually feel repellent if it continued for many more pages than it does. The fact is that Eliot blinks—she rescues Dorothea by having Casaubon die an early death. In doing so she avoids having to play out the terms of the terrible conflict she's set up, but she provides huge relief to those of us who want Dorothea to be able to get on with her life.

It seems to me that the novel genre came to its fullest flowering when societies were still bound by a well-defined set of customs and ethics but were becoming open enough to allow for the recognition of individuals who were at odds with those customs and ethics. *La Princesse de Clèves*, published anonymously in France in 1678, is generally understood to be the first novel in the West to examine in detail the interior lives of its characters. The princess, a married woman in the French court, falls in love with a nobleman. The nobleman is also in love with her. Bred to faithfulness and honor, they do not reveal their feelings to each other, and their forbidden passion leads to death and the nunnery. The reader's sympathies are clearly meant to be with these two characters who cannot live within society's codes. Countless novels that followed took up the dissection of thwarted desire. Prohibitions produce drama, external and internal.

When social structures break down to the extent that they don't provide much pushback against individual desire, the novel breaks down a bit too. *Middlemarch* is perhaps the apotheosis of the society/individual equipoise in English literature. More broadly, it could be argued that this perfect equipoise began around the time of Jane Austen and continued through Wharton's *The House of Mirth* and Forster's *Howards End*. After that, the novel turned more deeply inward, toward the streams of consciousness of Woolf and Joyce, and became more fragmented. Today, if we want to experience narratives of densely connected and rooted communities, we often have to look to historical fiction, fiction from other countries, or fiction and narrative nonfiction from more insular subcultures. I recently read *Educated,* Tara Westover's riveting 2018 account of her upbringing in a religious survivalist family in Idaho. I would never want to live through the things Westover did—she was forbidden to go to school, and one of her brothers was repeatedly violent toward her— but as a writer I was awed by the wealth of her material: her manic-depressive father's hoarding and stockpiling of guns . . . her midwife-healer mother's home manufacture of herb tinctures . . . the dangerous scrap-metal yard where most of the family worked. Westover, like a Victorian heroine of old, has to struggle against the rigidity of her family's rules and structures, and suffers within her body and mind the rending of ties.

When I was a college student first encountering *Middlemarch*, I had no picturesquely or grotesquely restricting society to write within or against. My parents had raised me in a very hands-off manner, which allowed me a lot of freedom but also led to bewilderment and a sense of aloneness. My primary antagonist was my own mind, its inchoate fears and desires. I suffered less from conflict with a community than from loneliness. A 2020 *New Yorker* article by Jill Lepore claimed that the word "loneliness" rarely appeared in print before the year 1800. Citing the work of one historian, she wrote, "It's not that people—widows and widowers, in particular, and the very poor, the sick, and the outcast—weren't lonely; it's that, since it wasn't possible to survive without living among other people, and without being bonded to other people, by ties of affection and loyalty and obligation, loneliness was a passing experience."[5] In *Middlemarch*, Dorothea and Lydgate are indeed lonely and isolated in their marriages, having realized that they are immured forever with another human being who cannot even begin to understand them. The Reverend Farebrother, who is in love with Mary Garth but realizes that she prefers Fred, is another example of a lonely individual. Nevertheless, even the lonely in *Middlemarch* have deep ties and know where they belong (Reverend Farebrother, for example, is responsible for supporting his elderly mother, his sister, and his aunt), and that is surely one of its attractions for me as both a reader and a writer.

It's taken me a while to see the way in which all four of the novels I've published are very much about loneliness: my first, *The Understory*, the most so. *The Understory*'s protagonist, Jack Gorse, is a forty-year-old ex-lawyer who lives on pennies in a rent-controlled apartment on

Manhattan's Upper West Side. His life consists of reading and walking the city; he is outside what we might call the productive economy. He has no friends and no family. When I was in my late teens and early twenties, I romanticized aloneness, thought I wanted it. I imagined that if I could read and write all day, I would live in a kind of self-sufficient bliss. I believed that solitude was the only way to get at deep truths about myself and the world. But in fact too much solitude was killing me; I was not nearly as suited to it as I thought. *The Understory* is also about compulsiveness—a trait I have tendencies toward—and how it both arises from and exacerbates aloneness. Fundamentally, *The Understory* is a fable in which I, now a married person with children, displaced both my longing for and horror of solitude onto another character, exaggerating them to an extreme. Just as Eliot plays out self-indulgence versus self-repression in *Middlemarch*, I played out solitude versus connection in my own novel.

My three other novels also feature isolated characters. In *The Virgins*, the female protagonist, wholly absorbed in her anxious self-inspections, is unable to believe that anyone sees and accepts her, while the narrator considers everyone else to be either superior to or beneath him, and therefore is connected to no one. *Eleven Hours* focuses on a woman who, family-less and having split up from her fiancé a short time before, goes through childbirth completely on her own. The heroine of *Matasha*, my novel for tweens, is an only child who has to learn to cope with abandonment by her mother and her longtime best friend.

Are modern novels usually about loneliness to some degree? After all, they generally depict the struggle against obstacles to achieve some sort of goal or identity. Obstacles throw one back on oneself and emphasize one's separateness and uniqueness. Frank O'Connor's much-cited book about the short story form, *The Lonely Voice*, argues that short fiction is about the isolated individual, while novels depict people more integrated into communities. But at the very least, novels acknowledge the problem of the tension between our aloneness and our ability to be known.

Before I wrote my published books, I made a couple of attempts to write a big, Eliot-esque novel depicting different social strata and their intricate interweaving. I abandoned these before very long. My attempts to reproduce Eliot's magisterial, confident, richly subclaused style probably resulted in howlers (I threw out those pages long ago). Just for starters, I didn't have her powers of observation or ear for speech or deep psychological understanding. Even if I had, the microcosm novel is a stretch for writers today. We have simply become too far-flung, too diversified, to novelistically encompass any particular society at any given time. To my mind, the contemporary works that come closest to doing so have been story collections. Edward P. Jones's *Lost in the City* and *All Aunt Hagar's Children* and Elizabeth Strout's *Olive Kitteridge* make Washington, DC, and the fictional town of Crosby, Maine, feel universal in somewhat the same way Eliot does Middlemarch. Both feature communities that are more rooted and interdependent than is usual in America: *Olive Kitteridge* because of Maine's remoteness and sparse population; *Lost* and *Aunt Hagar's* because of the lack of economic mobility in DC's African American community. But while Jones's stories in particular often employ a distant and omniscient narrator, neither Jones nor Strout uses one as boldly explanatory as Eliot's.

Not having grown up in a tightly knit community, I couldn't feel community in my bones the way one needs to—or at least I would need to—in order to write about it. My material was going to have to be different. The most successful pieces of fiction I wrote during my early adulthood, some of them merely fragments, others closer to poetry than to fiction, were about single consciousnesses and states of extreme feeling more than action and the interplay of characters. That was where the juice was for me. Not only did my friends and workshop colleagues find them more effective, I found them more engaging to write.

One of these early pieces featured an encounter between a prostitute and an American traveler in a German hotel. I have no recollection of how I came up with this scenario. The point of view was the prostitute's, and the focus was her experience of intercourse with the man. When I think about it now, what lonelier situation could there be than a sexual encounter that is nothing but a financial transaction between two people who don't wish to know anything about the other and will never see each other again? I positioned my narrator at a great distance, emotionally, from the woman; this narrator had access to her innermost thoughts but described them clinically. This allowed me to access her sense perceptions, masochism, and buried rage without feeling threatened; the character felt at a safe remove.

Still, once it was finished the piece frightened me, and listening as another member of my workshop read it out to the group was even scarier. I didn't want others to know how bleak the material I had in me was, how interested I was in this amoral, unpleasant scene. Everyone would now know that I was a perverse, angry, damaged person. Surviving that reading and, even more, receiving the enthusiastic praise of my fellow students, was a milestone. Riding the subway home afterward, I understood something. I had found the Other in myself, a mysterious, unrealized, not necessarily pretty side, a side that fiction could access and give language to. It wasn't all of me, and it wasn't inhuman—far from it. Nor did I need to act upon or draw conclusions from it; I just needed to make it vivid. I knew that on a very deep level I had liberated something in myself and would have less fear as a writer from now on.

Only much more recently did I learn from Rebecca Mead's book *My Life in Middlemarch* that George Eliot herself reported that "in all that she considered her best writing, there was a 'not herself' which took possession of her."[6] Perhaps all imaginative writers have to touch down to this not-self to do good work. And this means we may not be able to model ourselves in every way after our writer heroes and heroines.

There was one useful element, however, that I could have taken from Eliot's work, and for a long time failed to. Dazzled by the complexity of her characters and the high seriousness of her concerns, I overlooked how much melodrama Eliot, like most Victorian novelists, packed into her novels. They contain infanticide, child abandonment, discoveries of hidden parentage, domestic violence, drownings and near drownings, mysterious deaths, embezzlement, fraud. A major turning point in my own work came when I started buying and reading some of the writing self-help books I found at chain bookstores, the ones with titles like *Write Your Bestseller Now*. I'd been too much of a snob to look at those books before; I assumed their advice would be crude and useless. But in fact it was helpful. I'd written too much fiction that turned on a small psychological insight or supersubtle implication. If I had been a maturer writer, perhaps I could have gotten away with that; it's not that it can't be done. But in my case, the advice manuals finally got me to experiment with more *stuff* happening in my fiction, more big stuff. If I'd been properly attuned, George Eliot could have taught me that earlier.

Still, being who I was, born when I was, stylistically I was going to need other models for my writing besides Eliot. I began to find them: Eudora Welty, Christine Schutt, the William Trevor of *Reading Turgenev*, John Banville, James Salter, Virginia Woolf—and poets, many poets. The radical subjectivity and compression of modern poetry led to rhythms that felt more naturally mine, and these rhythms became roads to dredging my subconscious. My material, like it or not, was close to home: the body, sexuality, the struggle for psychological balance, the struggle to connect to another human being. From Salter I learned that the use of a character who stands outside of a drama between two others could enable me to import some aspects of Eliot's know-it-all narrator. In short, a third character who admits what he doesn't know about the others has opened up for himself the permission to speculate, to pronounce, just as Eliot did but as contemporary readers no longer readily allow. Such a character has already signed a disclaimer. From Woolf I learned, through painstaking imitation of *Mrs. Dalloway* and *To the Lighthouse*, how to construct a third-person narrator who was no longer in the novel but rather a hovering consciousness, floating in and out of the minds of a small network of characters, and how to represent these characters' thoughts in a more image- and metaphor-driven manner.

George Eliot never stopped being my favorite author, but I had to learn that my writing method is nearly the opposite of hers. Where she expands, I contract. Where she is centripetal, I am centrifugal. Where she is objective and analytical, I dream my way in.

Our task as writers is to discover the way we have to write.

NO MADNESS IN GEORGE ELIOT

NOT LONG AGO I WAS at a dinner that included an old friend of my husband's, someone who reads widely and thoughtfully. I mentioned to David that I was going to be writing a book on *Middlemarch*. Later, we were talking about the contemporary Irish author Colm Tóibín, a favorite of David's. David remarked, "Tóibín is the opposite of Eliot. In Tóibín, human motivation is impenetrable. Eliot is all about breaking it down, making it comprehensible."

Only days after this conversation, I came across a comment by the author and critic V.S. Pritchett that made a similar point. "There is no real madness in George Eliot," he wrote in his essay collection *The Living Novel* (1946). (He added that there was no madness in Victorian fiction, period, making an exception for *Wuthering Heights*.)

David's comment was more careful and exact, I think.

Eliot does "break it down," but that doesn't mean there's no madness in her world. It's simply that she is a genius psychoanalyst who can pry apart a multiplicity of motives and self-deceptions and show us why her characters do the crazy things they do. I get what Pritchett's saying: Eliot's not interested in the mentally ill or in flamboyant, extremely non-normative behavior. Irrationality, however, absolutely. The actors in *Middlemarch* continually make self-defeating choices, provoking and baffling neighbors and friends who, because they stand at a distance, can see these mistakes oh so clearly. But as Mrs. Cadwallader says (apropos of regretting that Lydgate hasn't made a better marriage), "It's no use being wise for other people." This is a line I understand infinitely better at age fifty-seven than I did at twenty. The ever-confident Mrs. Cadwallader means that *she* knows what's wise and just can't get other people to know it as well. I mean that I've come to understand that I don't know what is wise for other people, and am increasingly reticent about imposing my (supposed) insight on them. One of the ways to learn this humility most quickly is to watch your children move out of their teenage years into young adulthood.

Eliot absolutely anticipated Freud in her awareness of how little we comprehend about ourselves and others. She catches us out in our hypocrisies, our ill-founded grandiosity, our magical thinking. Peter Featherstone's relatives hang around his residence for days on end, waiting for him to die. Each is convinced Featherstone will favor him or her in his will. The richer relatives believe that he will reward them for managing their money so well: "They knew Peter's maxim, that money was a good egg, and should be laid in a warm nest." A poor relation reasons that since Featherstone never gave him money while living, he will certainly want to make up for that at the end. Another reassures himself that "blood [is] thicker than water," and Featherstone will have to be most generous to his nearest relations.

It all comes back to the flame and the mirror. Our built-in bias to see everything as relating to ourselves makes us misread most everything. A bloated self—ego— is our problem. Freud's therapeutic aim was to restore a cooperative balance between the id, the ego, and the superego—our primitive greed and lusts; our rational self; and our moralizing, punitive internalized voice—and Eliot's literary aims are similar, to shepherd her characters toward that livable balance between "complete self-repression and unchecked self-indulgence."

Most of them will not achieve it, but Eliot, from her

godlike perch, shows us the qualities they would need to do so. Really, she is showing us what we need—we readers.

I identify with many of the significant characters in *Middlemarch*: the spiritually striving Dorothea, the intellectually ambitious Lydgate, the vain Rosamond, the timid and life-denying Casaubon. (Sometimes, as I reread and reparse and re-edit my most trivial email communications, I think of that man.) There is another character I also identify with, and I feel the most uneasy about him, because he is a crook and case study in the pathologies of rationalization.

Nicholas Bulstrode marries into the world of Middlemarch: his wife, Harriet, is the manufacturer Mr. Vincy's sister. Bulstrode is a wealthy banker, religious in an ascetic vein, a teetotaler who lunches on water and a sandwich with ostentatious abstemiousness. He is also a philanthropist and the driving force behind the construction of a hospital that will employ Lydgate's new empirical methods. Yet no one other than Bulstrode's wife seems fond of him. His smug certainty about being an instrument of God's will puts off the live-and-let-live Middlemarchers. He is like Casaubon in his coldness and tendency to make those around him feel judged. And he does judge. He chides Mr. Vincy for the way he has raised Rosamond and Fred. When Lydgate, in debt, desperately approaches Bulstrode for a loan, Bulstrode refuses him, instead advising him to declare bankruptcy.

As it turns out, Bulstrode has a past life that, were it known, would drastically undermine his reputation in Middlemarch as an upright man. As an orphan, he was discovered to have a talent for preaching, and a prominent member of his church took him under his wing. He was brought into the man's pawnbroking business, which he came to recognize involved the fencing of stolen goods. When this benefactor died, Bulstrode married his widow, who in turn died and left him all her wealth. But Bulstrode knew his wife had an estranged daughter to whom the money should have gone. When he discovered this daughter's whereabouts, he kept quiet. At every step, he justified what he knew to be theft and fraud. All right, so the business he'd joined had some questionable practices—but he didn't set those up! All right, he'd kept money from his missing stepdaughter—but she'd been leading an immoral life, having run away from home to become an actress, and therefore didn't deserve the inheritance! With the money he came into, Bulstrode moved away to Middlemarch, where no one would be likely to learn his story. We will eventually find out, in a credulity-stretching coincidence, that Will Ladislaw is the son of the estranged daughter and the rightful inheritor of Bulstrode's assets.

Characters in Middlemarch rationalize their behavior all the time; however, Bulstrode's rationalizations involve wrongdoing that crosses the line into illegality. The more time that passes, the easier it is for Bulstrode to see his trespasses as unimportant. He convinces himself that God must approve of what he's done, since he's only been rewarded: with money, a devoted second wife, and an important position in the Middlemarch community.

The arrival of John Raffles forces him to confront his actions. The Raffles plot is confusing; every time I read *Middlemarch* I have to work out once again Raffles's past relationship to Bulstrode—he seems to be the one who found the widow's daughter and then was paid to keep quiet about it—and how he comes to reenter Bulstrode's life. The fact is that this part of the novel is not very vividly realized. Anyway, Raffles knows Bulstrode's secret. By this point he is destitute and an alcoholic. He comes to town and shakes down Bulstrode for cash. He leaves; he comes back for more. Finally, even though Bulstrode again gives him money, Raffles begins to tell whoever will listen semi-incoherent stories about the stolen inheritance.

Now Eliot grows masterful again. Raffles, suffering from the advanced stages of alcohol poisoning and raving about being chased even though he "kept his mouth shut," shows up at one of Bulstrode's properties, and Bulstrode, to remove him from the public eye, insists on having him stay there for medical treatment, allowing his housekeeper to believe that Raffles is an ill relative. He calls in Lydgate, who says that Raffles may pull through as long as he's not given alcohol. This would not have been the usual protocol of the time, which involved treating delirium tremens with the hair of the dog.

At first, Bulstrode obeys Lydgate's orders. We follow his silent hopes that Raffles will die and remove the threat of exposure hanging over him. Here, Bulstrode behaves like a good post-Freudian: he admits to himself his thoughts but strengthens his resolve to do what is right. There's no harm in just wishing for Raffles's death, after all. When Lydgate returns the next day to check on the patient, Bulstrode—suddenly anxious to have the doctor well disposed toward him—tells him he's changed his mind about the loan Lydgate requested; he's willing to front the money after all. That evening, turning over the care of Raffles to his housekeeper so he can get some sleep, Bulstrode forgets (or "forgets") to tell her when to stop administering the opium doses Lydgate has prescribed for Raffles's fits of terror. When he realizes this, he rationalizes that, who knows, since Raffles is still agitated, perhaps more opium is in fact necessary; really, who is to say? Not only does he not go to the housekeeper to correct the instructions, but when she comes to him later, reporting that Raffles is begging for a drink, he hands her the key to the liquor cabinet.

The next day, Raffles falls into a coma and dies. Lydgate is surprised but unsuspicious. Raffles is buried and Bulstrode feels, at last, safe. But soon the gossip mill starts to turn. Once townspeople hear the stories Raffles was telling shortly before his death, they suspect Bulstrode had cause to want to get rid of him. It is noted that Lydgate accepted money from Bulstrode in the midst of Raffles's final illness. At the next meeting of the board of Bulstrode's hospital, Bulstrode is called upon to explain himself, and when he can't, he is asked to resign. Lydgate is similarly disgraced.

The incremental path to Bulstrode's irrevocable act— the movement from terror to rationalization to decision making—is exquisitely detailed over fifty pages, giving an unparalleled view of the slow collapse of one man's morality. (Though it would be more accurate to say that Bulstrode's morality was never fully built, and the Raffles episode simply exposed it to the elements.) Every time I read the amazing passages about Raffles's death, I feel as if I were Bulstrode, and every time I am horrified by this fact. Do I suspect I am capable of passive murder? Am I likely to fence stolen goods? Cheat someone out of an inheritance? Thank goodness I've never been faced with such temptations; I pray I would never submit to them. And yet I understand every decision Bulstrode takes, and I can imagine taking them too if I were in his circumstances. It's not hard to find examples of my own rationalizations and hypocrisy. I am well aware that most of the ways I feed and clothe myself involve the slave-like labor of garment workers abroad and undocumented farmworkers here. I'm too lazy to find local farms that treat workers properly and too cheap to pay the premium for their goods. I swear off Amazon because of oppressive conditions in its fulfillment warehouses (and also because it bullies those who enable my livelihood, publishers), and then I cave and order from it again. Possibly I don't give as much money as I could to charitable causes. Bulstrode is a person who is protective of his advantages and ease. So am I.

But most of all what I relate to in Bulstrode is the fear of exposure. This fear is always there in his consciousness, but after Raffles's reappearance, it becomes a daily dread. I promise you that if you searched my past, you would not find any truly unforgivable acts. I shoved my brother once, in a rage, on a London Tube platform (not into the path of an oncoming train. Just on the platform). I have loudly berated friends. In my tightly budgeted twenties (all these things, I feel the need to mention, took place in my twenties), I occasionally nipped office supplies from my employer. I've sometimes paid people who cleaned my house or took care of my children not top rate but what I thought they would accept. I'm ashamed of all these things. Yet they don't seem to account for the pressing idea that I might someday be revealed to the world as . . . as what? Have I committed a shocking crime that I've somehow forgotten?

Maybe it's more simple than that. Maybe it's that I can be selfish and mean-spirited and know it, but don't want *other* people to know.

Eliot makes us feel Bulstrode's terror of punishment and ostracization, and this turns him from someone highly unsympathetic into a buffeted soul who is less foreign. He was an orphan, after all: he started life knowing the sting of not belonging to anyone. Eliot goes out of her way to say, "There may be coarse hypocrites, who consciously affect beliefs and emotions for the sake of gulling the world, but Bulstrode was not one of them. He was simply a man whose desires had been stronger than his theoretic beliefs, and who had gradually explained the gratification of his desires into satisfactory agreement with those beliefs." This is almost heartbreakingly generous. Eliot also makes it clear that Bulstrode married his second wife out of genuine love and has always been good to her. In the end, the thought of falling in her estimation is as piercing to him as the thought of rejection by the community. One of the most deeply moving passages in the novel occurs when Harriet finally learns about Bulstrode's past and his possible hand in the death of Raffles. First she privately grieves, mourning the disgrace to her family, and then she goes to her husband. He sees that she knows. "Her hands and eyes rested gently on him. He burst out crying and they cried together, she sitting at his side. . . . His confession was silent, and her promise of faithfulness was silent."

No matter what he has done, my heart goes out to Bulstrode, because I feel the tragedy of his unloved, unbelonging, undeserving state. And I am glad there is someone to stand by him and offer him comfort.

•

I don't remember thinking about Bulstrode when I wrote the character of Jack Gorse in *The Understory*, though he commits a terrible act—at least as terrible as Bulstrode's—and also rationalizes certain deceptions. For one thing, he lives nearly rent-free in his New York City apartment by pretending to be his deceased uncle. Because he spends his time studying the great thinkers of the Western tradition, he believes that working for a living is beneath him; he's owed this cheap apartment. Most of all, Jack does not know himself. He doesn't recognize his sexual desire for other men, but he probably wouldn't recognize a desire for women if he were wired that way. He has for so long repressed his need for human company that his personality begins to disintegrate when that need becomes too strong to resist.

Jack often misreads cues. He sees friendly overtures as threatening and unbearably intrusive, while at the same time developing a certainty that a casual acquaintance takes a deep and even romantic interest in him. Eliot writes over and over of the way imagination trumps reality in our lives, how we make the evidence fit what we want to see. We tell ourselves we are doing things for certain reasons when we're doing them for completely different ones. We see cause-and-effect relationships where none exist. As Eliot writes of Mr. Brooke, we are acute about the truths that lie on the side of our own wishes. Those that don't seem quite a bit more murky. Fiction could hardly exist without the troubles created by our astonishing inability to see life clearly.

I have a soft spot for the difficult souls in literature, the ones not easy to love. For the prickly, self-protective, often self-despising protagonists in the work of Alice Munro, Mary Gaitskill, Denis Johnson, Elena Ferrante, and Karl Ove Knausgaard, to name just a few. Reviewers called the narrator of my second novel, *The Virgins*, all sorts of bad names, "villain" and "psychopath" among them. I was startled, as I'd never seen him that way. Bruce Bennett-Jones is a damaged spirit who observes the love affair of two classmates with increasingly malicious envy. He clings to a feeling of superior pedigree (he comes from a family of prominent WASPs) because he believes himself personally inadequate. The main female character longs for connection and love, particularly sexual love, but her self-absorption and fear of her own brokenness get in her way. I agree with George Eliot that one of the greatest human tragedies is the fear of being known—specifically, the terror that if one is known, one will be rejected. For this reason (among others) I'm impatient with some readers' demands that fictional protagonists be "likable." A person who is afraid of herself and has therefore thrown up numerous defenses against becoming known is often not going to be hugely likable. Rather, she may be cold, dishonest, slippery, angry, violent, or self-destructive. Some of my own least appealing traits—an occasionally chilly reserve or emotional absence, a quickness to judgment—have surely resulted from a need to appear, to myself or to others, invulnerable, to be hidden behind a protective screen.

The character in *Middlemarch* other than Bulstrode who fights mightily against being known is Dorothea's husband, Casaubon. Although he has no past sins to worry about, he has gradually discovered that he isn't up to the task of completing his much-talked-up scholarly study. He is overwhelmed by his researches and consumed with memories of perceived slights from other religious scholars, determined to best them in the court of public opinion. Anyone who has ever been paralyzed by the need to write the perfect term paper can probably relate to Casaubon's state of mind.

About a third of the way into the novel, Eliot abruptly switches to a long passage giving us Casaubon's point of view. Until now we have seen him almost exclusively through the eyes of others. But as Eliot reminds us elsewhere, Casaubon has "an equivalent center of self, whence the lights and shadows must always fall with a certain difference." Now we learn of his naive ideas about women, his loneliness and anxiety, his intellectual insecurity, his fear of dying without ever having experienced happiness. Here and in other passages, Casaubon is associated with metaphors of duskiness and enclosure. He is "lost among small closets and winding stairs"; he lives in an "absence of windows" and "in an agitated dimness." Eliot describes his "small hungry shivering self" as "sensitive without being enthusiastic." And then she adds something unusual: "For my part I am very sorry for him." She is sorry because it is hell to feel nothing but one's own egotism and envy. It is hell not to connect with others. It's worth adding that after *Middlemarch* was published, when a friend asked Eliot whom the character of Casaubon was based on, she pointed to herself. This immensely loving and generous woman could acknowledge the parts of her that were frightened and closed off. Casaubon, a character who might easily be seen as contemptible—and has been, by too many critics—is in fact deserving of our empathy. He is a man who can't enjoy life and doesn't know why, is helpless to know how to change, and *feels* his deficiency. His self-awareness, however dim, is what raises his story into the realm of pathos.

Do characters such as Bulstrode and Casaubon evidence the presence of madness in *Middlemarch*? I suppose not, but their stories include unusual behavior that unsettles and outrages those around them. Casaubon, who has developed a dangerous heart condition, becomes convinced that Ladislaw, who has become friendly with Dorothea, wants to marry her for her money (completely untrue), and inserts a provision in his will that if the two do ever wed, she will forfeit any inheritance. The provision, when made public, soils both Ladislaw's and Dorothea's names by implying an improper relationship between them. Perhaps closer to madness is what Dorothea and Lydgate begin to experience in their marriages. Dorothea is pushed to the brink by rejection, and her life becomes "a perpetual struggle of energy with fear"— fear of her cold, controlling husband. Lydgate, discovering that the mild-seeming Rosamond is in fact one of the most stubborn creatures on earth, and implacably opposed to everything he cares most about, experiences helpless rages. I can't do justice here to Eliot's patient explication in each case of the resentment, loss of trust, and breakdown of communication that gradually lead to what she calls "the hideous fettering of domestic hate." "Domestic hate" is close enough to madness for me.

How did Eliot know such hate? When she wrote *Middlemarch*, she and George Henry Lewes had been married, in spirit if not in law, for seventeen years; by the time he died, they were together for twenty-four. It was a marriage filled with delight and mutual support. But Eliot had had the older, terrible experiences of bondage to and rejection by her father and brother. She knew that the people we are most intimate with can also be our destroyers. She knew that both connection and disconnection can unhinge us.

LOSING ONE'S NARRATIVE (I)

NICHOLAS BULSTRODE MIGHT HAVE CHOSEN morality over worldly advancement and did not. George Eliot clearly believes in free will—it is almost the foundation stone of her worldview—yet because she is so attuned to the tricks our minds play on us, she does not see free will as a simple matter. And because she recognizes how powerful external forces (luck, family, the community) can be, she certainly does not believe that we are contemptible if our will fails to triumph over all obstacles. She does not even believe it should triumph over all obstacles. I suspect she would think less well of Lydgate if he decided his wife's happiness no longer mattered to him and insisted she adjust to being the wife of a poor country doctor. He fell in love with Rosamond precisely because she was elegant, intensely feminine, and *comme il faut*; and he is honest enough with himself to realize this, as well as the fact that he unintentionally led her to expect a married life of material ease. I am certain Eliot would think less well of Dorothea if she left her sickly and dour husband to himself while she searched for charitable deeds to perform. Both Lydgate and Dorothea end up bending their strong wills to new purposes, ones they would not have chosen.

It cannot be an accident that the given name of Ladislaw, the poet-outsider who becomes Dorothea's second husband (his uncle Casaubon's prohibition making this an almost inevitable outcome), is Will. When he first appears, he seems a forerunner of a circa-1970s hippie: a drifter and dreamer, unclear about what he wants to do with his life. He studies art, he writes; none of it, apparently, with consistent effort. In a different way from Rosamond and Fred, there is the whiff of entitlement about him: his education and upkeep have been funded by his uncle, Casaubon, and he seems none too grateful for it.

Will expects a future of success—once he settles on a goal. Many of the characters in *Middlemarch* believe that success will be the outcome of the application of their will. Bulstrode channels his will (which he tells himself is God's) into gaining financial power and prestige. Lydgate believes his intellect and discipline will eventually lead him to scientific breakthroughs and a place in the annals of medicine. Rosamond expects to maneuver herself into a position in high society.

But the will, we learn, does not have a simple relationship to success. Lack of will is a problem (we see this in both the happy-go-lucky Fred Vincy and the "pulpy" Mr. Brooke), but so is will itself sometimes. "The mistakes that we male and female mortals make when we have our own way might fairly raise some wonder that we are so fond of it," writes Eliot. Several characters get just what they want and it doesn't make them in the least happy. Dorothea and Casaubon want and get each other, as do Lydgate and Rosamond. Many great novels, particularly the classics, are about characters either *not* being able to get what they want and dying tragically for its lack (this is the basic story line of *La Princesse de Clèves*) or getting it and presumably living happily ever after (see *Jane Eyre* and many Jane Austen novels). Eliot flips this script, giving her main characters what they want early on, and showing that what they wanted is precisely the problem to be worked through.

So is it just a matter of self-awareness? If we all saw ourselves more clearly, would we choose more wisely, and would all then be well? Not necessarily. Reverend Farebrother is too honest and too modest to interfere with Fred's chances with Mary Garth; he cedes the field to a man who is his moral and intellectual inferior. The result will be a continued lonely existence with the three female relatives he supports. Farebrother will always have the consolation of knowing he took the high road, but he won't necessarily have contentment.

Some characters in *Middlemarch* don't think so much in terms of success or failure, romantic union or disappointment, but nevertheless possess a fixed idea of self and future. Mrs. Vincy sees herself as the producer of good-looking and adorable children who will be admired and indulged by the world. Fred Vincy believes that he will always be happy and things will always go well for him because he's the sort of person that good things naturally happen to. Mary Garth, on the other hand, is "plain" and "early had strong reason to believe that things were not likely to be arranged for her peculiar satisfaction." Her life narrative involves having to settle for less than she would like. I believe Mary's name, like Will's, was chosen for a reason, conscious or unconscious. Mary Ann Evans was also seen as plain and possibly unmarriageable. (This was one of the reasons her father was willing to invest in her education.) It's one of the delights of the novel that Mary Garth is rewarded with its most satisfying marriage (to Fred, once he reforms his ways): not a flashy one, but one rich in love and companionship.

Every significant character in *Middlemarch* has a narrative he tells himself about who he is and how his life will take shape. As do we, the livers of real life. And how agonizing it is when we see evidence that our narrative is not unfolding the way it is supposed to. Instead of being favored by fortune, we don't inherit money we expected to, and we lose what little we have on a bad horse trade (Fred). Instead of living out our life as a feared power broker, we are run out of town (Bulstrode). Instead of becoming indispensable to a brilliant and benevolent husband, we find we are superfluous, suspected, and unloved (Dorothea). Instead of being a respected and successful novelist by the age of thirty, we have drafts of boring, partially finished stories abandoned in a file cabinet (Yours Truly). Where can we turn when this happens, what can we do?

In a foreshadowing passage about Lydgate as a young man, two lines have always strongly affected me. Eliot writes that "in the multitude of middle-aged men who go about their vocations in a daily course determined for them much in the same way as the tie of their cravats, there is always a good number who once meant to shape their own deeds and alter the world a little. The story of their coming to be shapen after the average and fit to be packed by the gross, is hardly ever told even in their consciousness." Shapen after the average and fit to be packed by the gross! At this point I always visualize a carton of eggs (that's a dozen, not a gross, but no matter).

At fourteen, if you coaxed me, I might have admitted that I planned to one day be notable, a household name. It wasn't just that I had always been one of the smart kids in school. At ten, I wrote a novel, about a slave girl escaping to the North with Harriet Tubman, that was later published by a small press. At twelve, I was selected as a cast member for a Chicago children's television program. But by twenty, encountering *Middlemarch* for the first time, I had aged out of being a wunderkind. My writing was no longer precocious. In high school and college I had gotten to know people obviously brighter and more talented than myself; about the only way in which I currently knew myself to be unusual was that I was seeing a therapist three or four times a week. I was still young enough for dreaming, but the "packed by the gross" passage hit a nerve. I feared that being one in a soldierly line of identical eggs could in fact be my fate.

Back when she was Mary Ann Evans, George Eliot knew the dread of her ambitions and ideals sputtering out to nothing, of getting lost in a provincial backwater, overlooked and unappreciated. She was sixteen when her mother died and her formal education ended. She left boarding school and took over as her father's housekeeper, first near Nuneaton and then in Coventry. Coventry was home to a small group of intellectuals who questioned the beliefs and practices of organized religion, and Mary Ann fell in with them. Visitors to this circle included sociologist-activist Harriet Martineau and Ralph Waldo Emerson. Over the next years, even with her family obligations, Mary Ann managed to produce a translation into English of an important German work on the life of Jesus, which contested the idea that Jesus had performed any miracles.[7] She must have yearned for a full-time life of the mind, a chance to test her capabilities. But, like (we shall see) Dorothea with Casaubon, or Lydgate with Rosamond, Mary Ann believed her allegiance belonged to someone else, and she remained with her father. Given her increasing differences with him about religious observance, the relationship was at times extremely painful to them both.

At the same age that Eliot was looking after a family member, I was attending an excellent boarding school and then an excellent college. I had opportunities she never dreamed of. I worked on the college literary and feminist publications, found I liked the process of putting them together, and after graduating applied for jobs in magazine editing. During these years I felt shaky emotionally, to be sure, even though psychoanalysis and the passage of time were gradually working in my favor.

My eating disorder, which slowly lessened its hold on me, had originally developed toward the end of high school as a simultaneous compulsion to restrict my eating and to binge on "forbidden" items like ice cream and candy. I was afraid of becoming "fat" and horrified by the experience of not being able to control my own behavior. I'd always been proud of my will, the way it enabled me even as a little kid to stick to plans such as teaching myself to type or completing a charitable walkathon of several miles. And suddenly, at the age of sixteen, it could no longer be trusted. After a year or so with my analyst, I'd been able to stop bingeing, but the idea of losing control remained a specter for a long, long time. A different manifestation of it was my great terror of mental breakdown. For reasons I've never completely understood, I pictured myself as walking a very narrow cord of sanity above a yawning abyss. Little things threatened my equilibrium enormously. If I couldn't have some item of food I wanted, when I wanted it, I went into paroxysms of anxiety. There were times when, after making plans with someone, I *could not* join them, because . . . because . . . I didn't know why, but I simply couldn't. Occasionally I was unable to fight off a sadness so drenching that I couldn't speak in company and had to make an awkward and disruptive departure. My emotions were inconveniently always too apparent on my face—once, a total stranger called out to me on the street: "Hey! It's not so bad!" Like Dorothea's, my days seemed to be "a perpetual struggle of energy with fear." I was ashamed of my brittleness, and didn't want anyone to know how close I was (so I thought) to insanity, or at least a total breakdown of healthy functioning. In retrospect, it's hard to know whether I was really so at risk. I went faithfully to my classes, wrote all my papers, got up every morning for work. The terror was real, but maybe terror was all it was.

My narrative at that time, and for many years to come, was that I was a sick person who was trying to pass as healthy, that I was disastrous at relationships, even friendships, and that I might end up lonely, mad, and locked up in some institution. I had friends, even good ones, but the closeness and trust I longed for was elusive. I was too ashamed of my eating problems and my deep feelings of unhappiness to confide about them. As for romance, the problem wasn't in the kind of partners I chose. I've always been attracted to kind and reliable men and have never understood the fabled magnetism of bad boys.

In an essay called "Education of the Poet," Nobel Prize–winning poet Louise Glück wrote of her teenage anorexia and its accompanying "extreme rigidity of behavior." There was a lot of rigidity in my nature too. When my routines and my control over time or food were threatened, I responded with anger, which was really masked panic. I was thin-skinned and judgmental. I convinced myself of innumerable flaws in the men I was seeing, and sometimes broke up with them as a result, only to feel the loss terribly. If I didn't engineer the breakup, the relationship eventually collapsed under the weight of its own misery. I saw all this and yet felt helpless to change it. (Let's put it this way: I could not control my excessive need for control.)

On the outside, my life continued on unremarkably. Like Lydgate building his practice in Middlemarch rather than London, I got a job after college graduation at a local Connecticut publication so I could continue my analysis, and tried not to be too envious of friends moving on to higher-profile places like the *Village Voice* and *Vogue*. I stayed in New Haven for two and a half more years, having parlayed my editorial assistant job into one as staff writer. In my free time I wrote a play about Henry James's emotionally disabled younger sister Alice (ahem). By the time I turned twenty-four, I was beginning to feel I could handle life without my analyst, and he thought so too. I moved to New York City, first working at a hip downtown weekly and then at the more staid *Glamour* magazine. I revived my fiction-writing ambitions by joining a workshop. But gradually, over the months, I was sliding into a depression. It took so much work to stay on an even keel, to handle the continued anxiety around food. I had no romantic partner and wasn't optimistic that if I found one, that person would put up with me for long. Happiness was never going to come my way, was it? Clearly I was incapable of it.

Scared by the depression, I did what I could. I found myself a new therapist. I signed up for a women's self-defense course—the idea being to address my feelings of powerlessness and productively channel my rage (it helped). I agreed to go out on yet another date my mother had set up—and it turned out I liked the guy. J and I had some stops and starts, but over time I could see that I truly enjoyed myself with this funny, smart, and affectionate man. Maybe I was just ready, just a little more elastic in my thinking and behavior, a little less frightened by everything. J made me laugh. Sometimes he made me laugh at myself—*that* was new! Sometimes I even made him laugh.

J liked to do things. He coaxed me into hiking and canoe outings, fishing, and days at the beach. Used to my very regulated, homebody-ish habits, I could get agitated and restless during these trips, desperate to go home, but somehow I always wanted to join him more than I wanted what was familiar and solitary. My life was opening up; J's enthusiasm and enjoyment were infectious. Astonishingly, little by little, I was becoming a more spontaneous, happier person. J and I knew how to fight, too, and did it a lot, always working our way back to understanding before parting or going to bed. I began to know what it was like to be in a relationship that felt stable and nourishing. After a year and a half, we moved in together.

This summary makes the trajectory sound rather fast and sure. It didn't feel that way at the time. I dealt with worries and crises at my job, got a promotion, wondered if I was wasting my life by not writing more, sweated over assignments in my fiction workshop, remained obsessive about what I ate and when, had cycles in which a low mood pulled me down and I had to spend days crawling back up again. But small positive steps added up. By the time I was twenty-eight and J and I were engaged, my narrative went like this: *I have a respectable job where I am well thought of, have found a good man; I believe in happiness and think things will continue to get better all the time; one day J and I will have children and raise them in a warm, busy home; we'll spend plenty of time in nature. And maybe I will even publish some fiction.*

I can't be sure what led me to reread *Middlemarch* the year I was thirty-one. I think it was seeing a pretty, clothbound Everyman's Library edition, with a ribbon for a marker, at one of the bygone independent bookstores in our Upper West Side neighborhood, Endicott or Shakespeare & Co. I've always relished the tactile qualities of books (I appreciate the convenience of e-books but can never get quite as immersed reading one), and from time to time I would obsess over spending some precious discretionary funds on a certain edition, going back repeatedly to a bookstore to skim and handle it until I finally gave in. Having bought this new *Middlemarch*, I needed to justify my purchase by reading it.

Once again I was transported into a dream of compassion and clarity, and was even more painfully pierced by Lydgate's story of thwarted ambition.

The chapter that contains the passage about being shapen after the average and fit to be packed by the gross—chapter 15—is entirely taken up with an account of Lydgate's life before his arrival in Middlemarch. It's a tour de force that leads us to know Lydgate more comprehensively than any other character in *Middlemarch* (we may go deeper into Dorothea's psyche, but we know more *about* Lydgate). Eliot is lavish in her attention to him. We learn that when quite young he stumbled across an old encyclopedia and was fascinated by the pages on anatomy. We learn of his studies in London, Edinburgh, and Paris, his susceptibility to the charms of women, the direction of his interests in research. Eliot invokes Xavier Bichat, a French pathologist who at the turn of the nineteenth century theorized that the organs of the body were not wholly independent entities but rather made up of interconnected tissues. Lydgate believes there must be an element common to all these tissues and intends to discover it, making use of a microscope, which Bichat did not. We also hear of Lydgate's dramatic, even frightening, flirtation in Paris with a French actress who murders her husband one night in an onstage "accident" at which Lydgate is present. After this adventure, Lydgate swears off romance for the foreseeable future.

But not long after Lydgate moves to Middlemarch, he is bewitched by the lovely Rosamond. He finds himself engaged to her without knowing exactly how it happened. He thought he was merely passing the time with a pretty and agreeable woman, but she believes he has serious intentions, and when she begins to suspect otherwise, weeping before him in disappointment and shame, he is so remorseful that he ends up proposing. (Another of fiction's great ill-advised marriages, Pierre and Hélène's in *War and Peace*, is also the result of a man feeling too embarrassed to admit he's not really interested.)

Lydgate and Rosamond's union is an outstanding example of Eliot's ability to show that the road to marital hell, like many life paths, is traversed in incremental steps. Lydgate has been raised in an upper-crust family and has all the markers of his class: the education, the self-assurance, the dress. The Vincy family and others assume he is well off, but his pedigree has left him more in the way of manners than money. He has enough to meet his few needs when he's a bachelor, but once he is married his funds are rapidly depleted by the purchase of a home and diversions for Rosamond. Rosamond expects to be provided with the "right" things and Lydgate, never having learned to penny-pinch, doesn't quite realize how much the right things can end up costing. He also has expected that his Middlemarch practice will be more lucrative than it turns out to be. The established doctors in town bad-mouth him, offended by his fancy education and principled refusal to sell medications. Potential clients are put off by his association with the much-disliked Bulstrode and his new hospital. Lydgate soon finds himself in debt and his wife blaming him for it—he must be managing business poorly.

From almost the beginning of the marriage, Lydgate realizes that he is overmatched by Rosamond, and "secretly wonder[s] over the terrible tenacity of this mild creature." He'd assumed that with his education and intellect, he would be the deciding force in their household; he now sees these are impotent against her settled opinions and aims. Neither argument nor affection ever cause her to yield. She may love Lydgate, but that doesn't change her demands one bit. His research ambitions are meaningless to her, a mere obstacle to material reward and status. She wants to move to London, where surely a better sort of clientele will solve all their problems. For Lydgate, this would be a terrible defeat; he's invested a great deal both financially and emotionally in his Middlemarch practice.

So Lydgate learns to hide any difficulties from his wife. He gives in on smaller and then larger matters, but eventually he is forced to ask Rosamond to economize. She responds as if personally offended. In secret, she approaches a wealthy uncle of Lydgate's, sure of charming him into a monetary gift, and is startled when she is rebuffed. Lydgate is enraged when he learns what Rosamond has done—he is a man of great pride—and crushed by her unwillingness to see their troubles as something they will face together. He is also exhausted by professional rivalries. The marriage becomes a standoff, with each partner feeling wounded and misunderstood, harassed and alone.

In the end, as we know, Lydgate gets entangled in the Bulstrode fiasco. When the story of Raffles comes out, the town believes that the loan from Bulstrode was hush money. Lydgate's reputation is ruined, and Rosamond gets her wish to move to London, where they can start over. One could say that Lydgate's life narrative came up against Rosamond, and Rosamond won.

The coda to Lydgate's story is sad. He gains "an

excellent practice" divided "between London and a Continental bathing-place." Eliot is amusing herself here. Lydgate specializes in gout—a rich person's disease—and the "Continental bathing-place" is where he can serve his wealthy patients during the summer season. He is still skilled and kind, and in his new life he is valued and trusted, but he also has abandoned his researches and "always regarded himself as a failure; he had not done what he once meant to do." Rosamond is, of course, a great social success, considered delightful by everyone. Lydgate dies early, at fifty, of diphtheria. We are given to understand that while their marriage eventually settles, there are always deep currents of disappointment and resentment underneath. Lydgate once calls Rosamond his basil plant, "and when she asked for an explanation, said that basil was a plant which had flourished wonderfully on a murdered man's brains." (I find this one of the funniest lines in the book.) We can remember here the warning story of Lydgate's early Parisian love, who did in fact murder her husband. Anyway, no need to worry about Rosamond: she gets remarried to a wealthy man with whom she continues to raise her four daughters.

Lydgate's fate has always haunted and yet reassured me. He does not become small, mean, or bitter (okay, he is a little bitter). He does worthwhile work (even medicine for wealthy people is worthwhile), produces a treatise in his specialty, and fathers children. He is a failure by his own lights, but I think Eliot judges him more generously. By the time I was a young married person, rereading Lydgate's story, I too knew there was life beyond the disappointment of not achieving one's highest ambitions. Like Lydgate, I was perhaps serving mammon, by working for a glossy magazine full of makeup and relationship advice. Shouldn't I be at, say, *Harper's*, editing intensively reported pieces on foreign wars? But I had a life. I got up in the morning, did my often interesting work—I liked those relationship pieces—spent time with someone I loved. And unlike Lydgate, I wasn't boxed in. My job left me time to write, and I *was* writing.

In the passage on Bichat and his tissue theory, Eliot drops a hint about Lydgate that could easily be missed. She writes: "What was the primitive tissue? In that way Lydgate put the question—not quite in the way required by the awaiting answer; but such missing of the right word befalls many seekers." We're not told exactly what is wrong with the way Lydgate conceptualizes his search, but we're tipped off that he may be a sort of Casaubon, following a dead-end line of inquiry. And of course much scientific research, even research carried out over decades, doesn't lead to the discovery of important truths. But I think pursuing a false hypothesis would still have been a happier fate for Lydgate. He would have had the dignity and pleasure of working toward a goal he felt significant, and perhaps of showing other researchers paths that might now be avoided.

I had the happiness of my own pursuits now, even though their outcome was uncertain. I did some book reviewing for newspapers and literary journals, contributed pieces to the magazine that employed me. In my fiction-writing classes, I worked hard and meticulously on my assignments, sometimes thinking back to what a natural I'd been as a kid. When had the naturalness disappeared? Why were the stories I now wrote often so mannered and inert? Why, when I felt so much, did so little of that feeling get conveyed on the page? I loved all sorts of fiction, from the classic to the experimental, but I still wanted most to write in the style of the great realists. They had the most breadth, I felt, the most to say about human existence. But whenever I tried to imitate, say, Jane Smiley in two novellas that had knocked me out, *The Age of Grief* and *Good Will*, my writing became—this was the feedback I got—flat. What I thought was transparent and mimetic was merely dull. It was only when I discovered authors like John Cheever and Eudora Welty, whose work often seemed opaque to me at first, who took more effort to read and felt at times artificial or too "done," that something began to happen in my own prose. I would write exercises in which I literally imitated the openings of a Cheever or Welty story word by word, inventing my own situations but then placing a noun precisely where, say, Cheever placed a noun and an adjective where he placed an adjective. It was heaven to feel the complex musical rhythms of a Welty story flowing out of my own fingers, appearing in markings on my own screen. I had always written a great deal by ear, and these masters taught me something about the infinitely varied heartbeats of sentences and helped me unearth the words to say what I wanted to say. My writing teacher, talking once about Isaac Babel, some of whose greatest stories are only a few paragraphs long, said that it was better to have written one line of connected prose than a stack of ineffective pages. By "connected" he meant that indefinable quality that gets across, that punches the reader in the gut with an experience of genuine recognition and emotion. I was deeply impressed by this statement. I dedicated myself to building connected work, sentence by sentence. I began to think of my ambitions in terms of years, not months—in terms, perhaps, of infinite time. It didn't matter if I didn't publish, as long as I could create sentences that were true and alive. Writing was about process above all.

I still believe this. And believing it, truly committing to it, may have been what eventually enabled me to publish: a small handful of stories that were rather prose-poem-y, and a few pieces that might have been called poetry but were labeled as fiction. I'd learned an enormous amount from studying poetry in my workshop too. I was thrilled by publication and yet sorry that my stories were a little . . . obscure. They weren't stories I would necessarily read if I were flipping through the magazines in which they appeared. They took a certain amount of work. Like many people, I was drawn most of all by plot and character. I still really did want to be Jane Smiley or Alice Munro. Or George Eliot.

LOSING ONE'S NARRATIVE (II)

THE THIRD TIME I READ *Middlemarch*, I was a mother of two, living in the New Jersey suburbs. The local book group I belonged to always chose a big book in the summers, giving ourselves ten weeks to finish it instead of the usual four. That summer of 2005, I suggested we do *Middlemarch*. I wanted to feel again its excitements and grandeur, and to see how the novel—or I—might have changed over the past decade.

I wish my diaries contained more notes about this third encounter. All I have are a few comments under the "Books Read" section I keep at the back of each current notebook. I wrote: "I am reading it quickly, for pure pleasure, as an entertainment, letting myself simply be filled with all its life and largeness of vision & generosity & humor & not worrying out every sentence. I didn't *worry* it on previous readings, but I sipped it, like a rich drink that had to be savored in small amounts. Now I'm just going bang-straight-ahead & loving it. This time around I finally see Lydgate—my favorite character—as a little less noble & romantic. I glean a bit more the 'commonness' (but so understandable!) Eliot speaks of in him."

Apparently, age (I was forty-two now) had made Lydgate less of an erotic dream object and exposed something I'd missed on previous readings. I'd never really understood what Eliot was referring to when she spoke of Lydgate's "spots of commonness," which she does in that long explanatory chapter 15. But Eliot is not hiding her meaning. She makes it clear that these "spots" have quite a bit to do with Lydgate's attitudes about women. At one point, when Lydgate is studying a new book on typhus late into the night, she jokes that he brings much closer and more probing attention to this reading "than he had ever thought it necessary to apply to the complexities of love and marriage, these being subjects on which he felt himself amply informed by literature, and that traditional wisdom which is handed down in the genial conversation of men." Lydgate arrogantly assumes he has nothing to learn about heterosexual love and companionship. Once again he is not all that different from the very different-seeming Casaubon in assuming that a wife exists to make a man's life comfortable and flatter his self-image. Lydgate's intelligence and emotional warmth made it hard for me to notice and remember his sexism. He's a man of his time (and of many times since).

Other than my new reaction to Lydgate, I remember only a few particulars of this third reading. I was moved as always by Dorothea and Bulstrode, and I delighted in sharing my enjoyment with seven other women who were enthusiastic about the novel and eager to discuss its minutiae. I was struck again by the fact that although I often found lengthy contemporary novels padded and undisciplined, there were no longueurs in *Middlemarch*. Every paragraph was engaging in itself and had a role to play in building the world of the town and its complicated inhabitants.

The main thing in my life that had changed since my previous reading, of course, was that I had become a parent. *Middlemarch* doesn't have a lot to say about children. There are glimpses of Mary Garth's youngest siblings, who are charming and very natural. Eliot wrote wonderfully about children, for instance the sister-brother pair of Maggie and Tom Tulliver in *The Mill on the Floss*. But in *Middlemarch* her focus is elsewhere, so much so that the early years of many of her significant characters are a blank. Dorothea and

Celia's parents are mentioned only briefly at the very start of the novel, and the girls' early loss of them seems to have left them oddly unaffected.

My own childhood took place at a time when, quite to the contrary, early experiences were believed to shape pretty much everything about a person. It was an era before a new wave of interest in genetic and biological causes of behavior, before the widespread use of psychotropic medications to alter brain chemistry. Nurture mattered far more than nature. And that, whenever I thought about having children myself, was daunting.

Parenthood—whether and when—was the main issue J and I had had to sort out before deciding to get married. J definitely wanted kids. I thought I wanted them, but avoided any precise commitment. "I'll have them when I'm forty," I pronounced. That wasn't good enough for J. He was six years older than I, for starters, and wanted kids while he still had plenty of youthful energy. He liked children a lot, was very good with them (he'd become a kind of benevolent uncle to my two-year-old half brother), and didn't see any reason to wait so very long.

I was afraid, though—afraid that I might not have the patience or self-denial required. I wondered if I could really be sufficiently loving and present for young children. That was of utmost importance to me: the feeling of emotional detachment that I associated with my own childhood was something I was determined not to pass on. I knew J would be a good parent. But what about me?

Gradually, I began to feel confident that I could be one too. I had strong memories of experiences and feelings from my own childhood and a great deal of respect for children, who it seemed to me were routinely condescended to and emotionally manhandled by the ex-young. More and more I was fascinated by babies and longed to hold and snuggle the infants of friends. I knew I wanted a life with J, and I now saw that life as including children. The urge for them became physical, primal.

And so, a couple of years after marrying, J and I took the leap and added a child to our home. We added two, in fact, in close succession. I left my magazine job after the first was born: I didn't see how I could be a mother and have a job and write fiction. I could do two of those things, perhaps, and the child was a given. So it was between the job and the fiction, and I was lucky that J could support our new family on his salary alone.

•

Motherhood, as it turned out, made me feel stronger and more centered than I had ever felt before. For the first time it was truly essential to put someone else's needs before my own, and I discovered that doing so made life vastly more meaningful. I had a role—what I did mattered. In my twenties, I'd probably been right to worry that I wouldn't have the patience for children, but now I did have that patience. My children's small bodies, their eyes full of light, their delighted laughter, their first teeth/steps/words/hugs—all these were deep, deep joys for me. I remember responding to the "I'm awake!" cry of one or the other child in the mornings, walking into a room to meet outstretched arms and an impatience to start the day! It seemed to me that my children were ablaze with consciousness, all systems switched to Go. It was beautiful, enlivening—inspiring.

And it was hard work. Having two kids within nineteen months of each other was exhausting at times, and I would be the first to say that the patience and self-denial I felt proud of were possible only because I had a certain number of hours of child care per week. I used those hours to nap, to exercise—and to write. Like many parents before me, I found that having a limited amount of time to work meant

I got down to it without foot-dragging. I'd never forgotten Casaubon and his sorry death surrounded by the endless disorganized notes of a never-completed project. I did not want to be that person, the one who was always going to write a book and never did, or did and then was too afraid to put it out there. In those years just before and after having babies, I'd finished some short stories, placed a few, and gotten many, many rejections. Sometimes those rejections were humiliating. But I was more ashamed of the idea of never even trying to publish. And so I clocked my time, day after day, and I blessed heaven and earth that we could afford child care, for both my sake and my children's. When I could get a reasonable amount of sleep and exercise, and write a little, I could be the kind of parent I wanted to be—felt I had to be.

And what kind of parent was that? Attentive, attuned to my children's responses, able to see through their eyes yet remain the outside, adult bulwark they needed. (Sort of like the position of George Eliot's narrator, as I've described it.) Generally I think I was all that. But looking back, I can also see how invested I was in the notion that my husband and I— but mostly I—could almost completely control our children's experience of life and their development. Could control, let's say, their narrative. Wasn't doing so, in fact, the core job description? I thought if I was always there to soothe them when they were afraid or hurt, if I was always empathetic and took their thoughts and feelings seriously, if I never readily let them feel that something I was doing was more important than they were, if J and I loved each other openly and created a family environment that was playful and fun, then our kids would grow up secure in the knowledge that they were loved, and would become confident, well-adjusted, and ethical human beings.

Be wary of narratives with "if, then" clauses, I would say now.

I don't think the goals I had (*be empathic; family life should be fun*) were bad ones. It's just that I was so afraid of any influences I couldn't manage. If we were visiting another home and the television was on, I was anxious that my kids would get exposed to something that would frighten them. (Vivid memories of my own TV-induced childhood terrors kept me alert about this.) If another kid was rough and mean, I thought mine would osmose obnoxiousness. If a babysitter was curt or neglectful, I believed my children would develop deep feelings of unlovability. In short, everything seemed to be at stake at all times. The kind of vigilance I developed took a lot out of me and maybe wasn't ideal for the kids either. It has taken me years to ask why I had so little faith in their resilience, in the existence of a margin for error. Was it because I myself, for whatever reason, had felt so fragile as a young person?

Control: again, that issue. I had been a child with a strong will and a lot of self-control. I was an adolescent with major control issues. And now my children were targets of my need for control. In some ways, oddly, I was a more laissez-faire parent than many of those I observed around me. It wasn't a big deal to me if my kids wouldn't eat certain foods, and I didn't care what they wore. I wasn't interested in changing their temperaments. I knew they had their own thoughts and opinions and didn't demand they accept mine. I didn't sign them up for a million extracurriculars—I figured time enough to get bored was good for a kid—or yell at them from the sidelines of their soccer games, desperate that they should make me look good. My preoccupations were pop culture, which I considered debased and a waste of time, and scary information that I didn't consider them ready for. I didn't intend to protect them from reality forever, but I figured the older they were before they got their noses rubbed in certain truths (death, explicit sex, violence), the better.

As far as I could see then, my highly involved and somewhat protective parenting worked. My kids were well behaved and affectionate, and they excelled in school. They laughed and were silly and confided their fears and feelings to us. They read a lot! One kid was socially anxious, but we figured that would pass. One kid could be stubborn and argumentative, but we could handle that. Kids aren't perfect, after all. When other parents complained about their children who acted out, who couldn't focus on their homework, or who played hours upon hours of video games, I just smiled sympathetically and felt a little superior. *I* hadn't let those bad habits develop.

In the meantime, I was gradually accumulating some publishing successes. The novel I started when the children were infants, and spent over two years trying to sell—*The Understory*—found a home with a tiny press. The next novel, *The Virgins*, got wider attention (leading to the reissue of *The Understory* by my new publisher), and I sold a third, *Eleven Hours*. Despite my lifelong diffidence in groups, I discovered there was one kind I liked: groups of other writers. With writers, I was miraculously less shy and fidgety. I loved hearing what they had to say, listening to them read their words, swapping complaints and insights about this crazy thing we felt compelled to do. This kind of community was extremely important to me, and helped me convince myself that I was not an imposter, that this writing thing I did was for real. That I had a place in life, not just as a wife and mother but as a person who worked with words. I was in my early fifties and publishing rewards had come late to me, but I was amazed they had come at all, and enjoyed them more for having had to wait so very long.

When I stopped to take stock, I felt . . . good! I could still remember the day when, out strolling my first, weeks-old child in the street, I found myself in a panic: this creature was going to be living with me *for the next twenty years.* The responsibility—the burden—seemed enormous. Well, twenty years had flown by—as the saying goes, the days had been long but the years were short. My kids had moved from elementary school to high school to college; they were, essentially, launched. They weren't without their problems, nor were my husband and I completely without ours, but it seemed as if I'd done it: truly and dependably rewritten that old, terrible narrative in which I ended up solitary, bitter, maladjusted, and on the margins of life. Instead I was happy, healthy, and financially comfortable, with friends I cared about. Moreover, I had fulfilled some long-held artistic goals and raised reasonably healthy children who would surely move on to fulfilling their own goals.

Whenever you've decided your story is fixed, you can be sure a new plot development will come along to challenge it.

It can be so hard to know when you have a child in trouble. The signs don't always come abruptly and unequivocally. I'm not going to go into much detail (and will conceal gender), for the sake of my kid's privacy, but their anxiety issues became pressing by late high school. We did what parents are supposed to do: found a therapist, got them on medication. They made a good adjustment to college at first, but later seemed, especially for a bright kid, to become bafflingly disengaged. We became aware of severe sleep issues. Later, after various attempts to cobble together a postcollege life, our child moved home, distressed and feeling defeated. There, under our noses, it was impossible not to see how the anxiety, ever mounting, had become paralyzing. My husband and I scurried to find a treatment program, new therapists. I was terrified and sometimes enraged at our child's unwillingness to get out of bed, to try to help themself, even as I understood that anxiety and depression drastically undermine willpower.

I felt consumed by my child's problems from the moment I woke in the morning until the moment I turned out the light at night. I lost my appetite and an unhealthy amount of weight. I fantasized horrendous outcomes that had more to do with me—with my catastrophic habits of mind when it came to my children—than with anything we had reason to believe would happen. But I was hounded by fear.

It's very painful to give up a narrative. It's very painful not to know what will happen, particularly when it involves one's child. My sense of shame went deep: I had fucked up parenting, I thought, either via something I'd done (too much protectiveness? too much indulgence?) or because of something I was (too anxious, a trait passed down through the genes?). I felt extremely alone.

It was just then that I began to read *Middlemarch* for the fourth time, in preparation to write this volume. No book could have been more of a balm. The thirty or so pages I read a day, over a period of two months, were an oasis, a refuge to which I could travel for order and calm. Again there were the stately, wise, generous sentences, the hidden nuggets of humor. Again there was the pleasure of following out one of Eliot's complicated thoughts to an unexpected conclusion. Again her narrator reassured me that for all my flaws, I was part of the human race, accepted, forgiven when necessary. Again I climbed inside the skin of others who were struggling and finding ways to make the best of their imperfect lives.

I was reading other texts, too, strictly for self-help, among them works by the American Buddhist Pema Chödrön and the "vulnerability researcher" Brené Brown. *Middlemarch* was strikingly in sync with these in its emphasis on the commonality of suffering and the need for people to be tender with one another. Like all genuinely disruptive events, my child's troubles were an opportunity to face universal realities I'd formerly kept at bay. In retrospect, the tightness with which I'd clung to my narrative of ever-increasing happiness was a red flag. A tight clutch is always a sign of fear and insecurity. The anxiety with which I attempted to control various influences over my children was proof in itself that I knew how often kids get into or experience trouble, how unavoidable is the fact that they will suffer. I was so afraid of the ways good fortune could be stolen from me and mine. What if my husband lost his job? What if that cyst on my ovary wasn't benign? Just as I'd been sure that my children could be ruined by a few bad turns, I was sure that I wouldn't be able to cope with any major reversals of fortune. And since I was sure, those things had better not happen. They couldn't happen. If you believe certain things *can't* happen, you have to do a lot of dancing to explain to yourself how it is that other people have massive heart attacks in their forties, lose their mobility to chronic illness, get fired, get divorced after twenty-five years of marriage, go bankrupt, lose a child. Each of these tragedies has happened to someone I know. But I still couldn't accept that any could ever happen to me.

It is very hard to have to admit that not all is well in your own marriage or family or psyche—but it also has the potential to make you feel less lonely. Shame is a large part of what creates the sense of aloneness—it's a throwback to the terrible and universal childhood experience of being punished or bullied, usually in a way that forces you to be literally separated from other people. You have to stand in the corner or go to your room, or all your classmates move away from you so that you're playing or sitting alone. It's visceral. My whole body shrank when I imagined people looking at me and thinking, "Pamela Erens? We thought she had it so together. Turns out she was a lousy mother." I could not bear anyone feeling sorry for me. But when from time to time I was able, despite my self-absorption, to talk with friends and neighbors and really hear *their* troubles, not comparing them to mine and deciding they were worse or better, when I observed that what those friends and neighbors told me did not make me think of them as losers or fuckups, I could glimpse the truth that heartache connected me with other people, rather than dividing me from them.

The arrival of the COVID-19 pandemic in early 2020 solidified this understanding. I was in a reasonably lucky category: as a healthy woman in my midfifties, I wasn't likely to die from the virus. My husband, in his sixties, would probably be all right too. Our children almost surely would be. But who knew for sure? For a couple of weeks in March, life changed at warp speed. The library shut down, the restaurants, then the schools. Did we need to wear masks or not? Sanitize groceries? Would we ever be able to find rice or flour again? There was so much that wasn't clear. What I did know—and knew more and more as the weeks went by—was that a lot of people would die, and even more people would lose their jobs and their ability to put food on the table. Both of my kids, currently unemployed, were going to be facing a much tougher job market than I had when I was in my twenties. A year ago, the idea of unusual obstacles for my children would have sent me into a spiral of worry and why-them-ism. Now this seemed to me to be the very definition of life: effort combined with stuff going wrong.

The commonality of misfortune and suffering is what Dorothea discovers, and helps others discover, in *Middlemarch*. At the start of the novel, she thinks of herself as a savior, someone who will *bring* improvement to others. In this way she is like Bulstrode, though with more heart. I've sketched in Dorothea's story already, but it would be useful to go into more detail about her character. There's a risk that I've made her sound a bit insufferable. She can be, at times. Not that long ago, my husband and I had a disagreement over how to handle a refund for a hotel reservation we weren't able to keep because an airline we'd booked an overseas trip on had gone out of business the very evening of our scheduled flight. After a drawn-out process, our credit card company reimbursed us for the hotel stay, but in the meantime the hotel had offered to apply our payment to a room if we made the trip at another time. My husband was considering accepting, but I thought being comped for a future stay after being reimbursed was double-dipping and objected. My husband, reacting more to my disapproving manner than to my position, told me, "Your moralism can be very high-handed sometimes." He saw some gray areas, pointing to the tens of hours he'd spent fighting with the credit card company and the fact that the hotel had said it would give us the room only if it was at a time when they had low occupancy. Our free room wasn't going to replace one that would otherwise have been paid for. I wasn't sure I agreed with his view, but the point was that I'd behaved as if even discussing the matter was beneath me—I hadn't at first even let my husband give his reasoning. I thought, "Oh, dear, I'm just like Dorothea at the beginning of *Middlemarch*."

But even at *her* most high-handed, Dorothea is also unpretentious, wholehearted, and loyal. I have always loved her for what Eliot calls "her usual openness" and her simplicity, the way she is incapable of gaming people or strategizing for effect. Her instant sympathy for others is a kind of superpower, although initially there are those who are omitted from its circle (Sir James Chettam, for example). Her marriage—the result of the unforgivable narrowness and triviality of her education, which leads her to idealize a man of learning—teaches her first that she is capable of error and, later, that even an oppressive husband has his painful vulnerabilities.

Dorothea's first reaction to losing her narrative—to finding out she is not in a story about being handmaiden to a Milton or a Pascal—is withdrawal, the usual result of such a loss. She is confused, then paralyzed, not knowing what to do with herself. When Casaubon's health begins to fail, she at least has a role to inhabit, as nurse, but her life becomes even more circumscribed. She has given up on the idea of playing Lady Bountiful to her parish, but in time she sees that there are people she can still help. They are not the faceless downtrodden but individuals she knows, or knows of, in her community.

When Lydgate is denounced by Middlemarchers for supposedly colluding in the death of Raffles, Dorothea becomes his sole defender. She argues to anyone who will listen that she doesn't believe he is capable of taking a bribe, and she goes to him to express her support. Lydgate, who has received no kind word from anyone, including his wife, is very grateful. Dorothea asks for his version of events and then gives him the money to repay the debt to Bulstrode so that he can disengage himself from the latter's affairs. An earlier version of Lydgate would never have allowed her to do this, but he has been humbled. Dorothea tells him she will rally support for him in the community. But most of all she makes it clear that she understands how bitterly ashamed he is to have stumbled in so many ways: in his marriage, in his work, in his research. "I meant everything to be different with me. I thought I had more strength and mastery," he confides. Dorothea's empathy is the greatest gift she has to give, greater than the building of better cottages for tenant farmers—though she would do that too if she could.

Later, Dorothea helps Rosamond realize how much Lydgate still loves her. Rosamond's single act of true selflessness occurs in this meeting. She has been flirting dangerously with the idea of an affair with Will Ladislaw, and crumbles when Will rejects her and makes it clear that Dorothea is the one he longs for, though he believes Casaubon's will makes their union impossible. (This is the moment in which Rosamond's own narrative is destroyed: before now, she has assumed she is the object of every man's desire.) As with Casaubon, literary critics tend to be very hard on Rosamond, seeing her as a narcissistic monster. But, no surprise, Eliot is more nuanced. While she often employs the word "shallow" in connection with Rosamond—the spatial metaphor is apt; Rosamond's emotions do not get fed by deeper springs of understanding and self-awareness— another used over and over, especially in the last pages of the novel, is "poor," as in "poor Rosamond." The phrase may be lightly ironic, but it is not sneering. Like Casaubon,

Rosamond is something of a tragic character for Eliot. Her inability to experience true vulnerability or to question her version of reality means that her experience of life is radically impoverished; she is shut off from intimacies and pleasures that most of the rest of us enjoy.

When Rosamond actually meets Dorothea, thinking to confront a rival, the latter's openness and kindness affect her markedly. Dorothea begs her—delicately, not saying directly that Rosamond is in danger of falling into adultery—to believe that Lydgate suffers from having made her suffer, that he cares a great deal for her happiness. Rosamond knows that Dorothea believes she and Will are conducting a secret liaison, and that it has cost Dorothea a lot to make an errand of empathy to the woman Will apparently prefers. In response, for once setting aside her pride and her need to be queen bee, she tells Dorothea about Will's true feelings, paving the way for their union. (A brief note on Ladislaw, on whom I've spent little time, and portrayed as a bit pretentious. He too is allowed to develop over the course of the novel. His strengths are his quick mind, his sensitive nature, the loyalty of his affections, and his recognition of Dorothea as a woman worthy of love. He becomes a good match for her, though not all readers have seen it that way.)

The compensation for the pain of losing one's narrative is the humility and compassion that bring us closer to others and that—and this is among Eliot's deepest beliefs—create genuine good in the world. Two characters in *Middlemarch* share an odd trait, that of believing more in the goodness of others than the evidence would support. These are Dorothea and Caleb Garth, Mary's father, who is constantly getting himself in trouble by trusting to the decency of men more self-interested than he is. Precisely because Dorothea and Caleb are so innocent in their expectations, other people sometimes, to their own astonishment, meet those expectations. Caleb is a primary force in moving Fred from selfish and lazy youth to maturity and responsibility. Dorothea saves Rosamond from chasing after adulation and compromising her marriage to Lydgate. Faith in humanity improves the world.

The other compensation for losing one's narrative is that we are reminded of the possibility of (more) change.

When I was younger, I believed character was static. My tendency toward withdrawal and my occasionally explosive temper—I'd once thrown a typewriter off a table in a fit of rage over a college boyfriend (he was not present)—were surely permanently disabling characteristics, proof of my inability to love anyone. What I was, or feared I was, was something I was doomed to forever.

Maybe this belief is more typical of the young, who don't have decades of experience to contradict it. Maybe when we're children it's more adaptive to assume the mean kids are always going to be mean, lest we end up like Charlie Brown, always having the football pulled away from us at the last minute. But it's a mistake not to see that while every human being has certain enduring tendencies, character is malleable and influenced by changing circumstances. My fatalism showed up in the fiction I wrote in college and my twenties. My stories' outcomes tended to be freeze-frame and bleak: someone wandering off into a future of enduring failure or despair. Failure was a favorite topic of mine. I wrote one story in which a gifted piano student intentionally plays the wrong piece at a competition, as a way of giving the middle finger to the teacher and parents who are highly invested in her success. (Failure *and* anger were favorite topics of mine.) At other times, I never even got to the ending of my stories, possibly because when you don't believe in character change, there's nowhere that interesting to go.

If I think about it, even my first two published novels unfold in a manner that doesn't allow my characters to change very much. They don't learn; they more just unravel.

In George Eliot, the possibility of growth and change is always a live concern. The novelist and academic Paula Marantz Cohen puts it beautifully: "Eliot seems to have conceived of human character as resembling a chemical reaction in which a large number of potentially important variables are present but only some are activated."[8] Depending on those variables, sometimes change comes too late to undo consequences; this is true of Lydgate. Over and over in the early sections of the novel Eliot speaks of Lydgate's pride and his belief in his independence. He simply can't see the ways in which he is vulnerable to forces outside himself. By the time he does, his life has been dismantled. Bulstrode's story is similar. His downfall is not so much because of the bad things he's done—Middlemarchers are fairly ethically flexible. It comes about because Bulstrode, out of fear of his own sinfulness, aggressively sets himself above others. He is rejected by the townspeople for his hypocrisy more than his misdeeds. What Lydgate and Bulstrode learn will probably prevent them from similar mistakes in the future, but they are permanently marked.

Other characters are fortunate enough to change before anything irreparable has occurred. Fred Vincy and Mary

Garth, now in their early twenties, were close childhood playmates, and neither has forgotten that when they were six years old, Fred "married" Mary by giving her the brass ring from an umbrella. Although Fred's parents consider the Garths beneath them socially, the Garths' house has always been a second home to him. For this reason, Fred's inability to repay the loan underwritten by Mr. Garth shames him deeply. The immediate result of Fred's fecklessness is that the money the Garths have painstakingly put aside to finance their fifteen-year-old son's apprenticeship, as well as everything Mary has saved from her work as an aide to the ill Peter Featherstone, will now have to go to pay off Fred's debt. Fred has always assumed that Mary will agree to marry him for real one day, but she says she won't accept him unless he stops hanging around with bad company and finds some respectable line of work. When she learns about the debt, she's furious. Fred tries to play on her pity—"You can never forgive me"—and she retorts: "What does it matter whether I forgive you?" Fred is still self-involved enough to be more focused on his own feelings than the damage done. It upsets Mary that Fred is content to nurture his worst qualities. She knows his decency and generosity and his affectionate nature, the "potentially important variables" that need to be "activated."

Perhaps seeing both his selfishness and his promise through Mary's eyes plants the seed of Fred's rehabilitation. Eventually he will gravitate to work that his parents look down on but that suits him (farming, under the tutelage of Caleb Garth), he will learn to work hard, and he will win Mary. It is not just that Fred has to learn to behave like an adult but that, like Lydgate, he has to learn that he is not a lone actor in the world, that what he does affects others and vice versa, that he is as vulnerable to folly and bad luck as the next person. In the coda to the novel we see Fred and Mary, white-haired and content in their old age, but Eliot never succumbs to the temptation to embalm her characters or her endings. "I cannot say that he was never again misled by his hopefulness," she writes of Fred; "the yield of crops or the profits of a cattle sale usually fell below his estimate; and he was always prone to believe that he could make money by the purchase of a horse which turned out badly." To return to Cohen's chemical metaphor, characters retain their basic elements, but a shift in the admixture can result in very different outcomes. I find this an extraordinarily hopeful philosophy.

The author Sarah Manguso's lovely book about keeping a diary has a title I cherish: *Ongoingness*. Manguso started her diary in her teens, she tells us, as an attempt to stop time, to preserve experiences that might otherwise be lost. As a lifelong diary keeper myself, I understand the impulse. But Manguso's diary consumed her, stealing from her life as she spent hours trying to record it. Later, especially after becoming a mother, she became more able to resign herself to the onrush of time, its ongoingness. Her students, she says, still fret about whether they will be successes at this or that; they are still preoccupied with the future, as young people tend to be. They still believe in the happy or unhappy ending. But Manguso says she "no longer believe[s] in anything other than the middle." We keep building narratives, but there *is* no narrative in quite the way we think.

Now more than ever before I have faith in the unexpected, as a fiction writer and as a human being. Whether a person's fate turns out to be good or bad—whatever those labels may mean (and we have an unfortunate tendency to judge an entire life by what happens nearest its end)—in the unfolding of that fate there is always wiggle room. A person, or a fictional character, may change slowly, over decades, or surprisingly quickly. Life is enduringly imperfect and continually in transition.

•

What do I see as *my* narrative now? I am trying to have

less of one altogether. I am trying to meet each morning without so much speculation. "Sufficient unto the day is the evil thereof," as the Sermon on the Mount informs us. In recent months I've seen a resilience in my struggling child that not long ago I feared I might not see. (Some potentially important variables have perhaps been activated.) I also know difficulties rarely evaporate into thin air. I don't think as far ahead as I used to, don't create beautiful pictures of a future in which all trouble has been airbrushed out. I will get there when I get there, and there will be challenges and—I trust—joys.

Let's tell the end of Eliot's story now. Her father died when she was thirty, giving her her freedom at last, as Dorothea gains her freedom when Casaubon dies. Soon after, Eliot—still Mary Ann Evans—left Coventry to travel in Europe with friends, staying abroad for several months. After a while, she found her way to London. She began to work, for little pay and without a byline, on book translations and articles for the *Westminster Review*. She got involved in more than one complicated and humiliating romantic situation with men who accepted her worship and then rejected her. Then she met George Henry Lewes. For bookish girls, the exquisite thrill of this story is that Eliot not only found love in the end but found it in someone who encouraged her to reach higher in her ambitions than she had ever thought herself to reach, and that in taking up the dare she succeeded beyond either of their wildest dreams, finding a channel for her gifts and leaving us works of permanent delight. Of course, Eliot's story is also a dangerous model. Eliot was definitely not "shapen after the average and fit to be packed by the gross"; she was a once-in-a-generation literary genius. Bookish girls like me have to be careful not to overidentify with her. And even as Eliot was one of the most admired and lauded figures of her time, we have to recall that her life was filled with sorrows. She was not always the calm and stately figure her portraits have immortalized. When young she was known for her emotional outbursts and even episodes of hysteria. She was ridiculed for her supposedly unfeminine looks, abandoned by her family, condescended to by male writer-rivals such as Henry James. She suffered from poor health and depression, and one of Lewes's children, whom she considered her own, died at the age of twenty-five from spinal tuberculosis.

Lewes passed away in 1878, after a short illness, at the age of sixty-one. Eliot, devastated, barely spoke to anyone for several months. Then, to the surprise of everyone, in the spring of 1880 she married John Cross, the Lewes's financial advisor, who was twenty years her junior. On their honeymoon, in Venice, Cross threw himself out a window into the Grand Canal, prompting speculation that the sight of Eliot's aging body—she was sixty—had triggered a nervous breakdown. One can hear the nasty, titillated snickers. (The incident remains mysterious. It is possible that Cross had become delirious from a fever. In any case, he survived, and later wrote a worshipful biography of Eliot.) Eliot herself died only six months later, and her reputation began a long downward slide, until a 1919 essay by Virginia Woolf restored her to a prominence that has rarely been challenged since.[9]

That is the external account of George Eliot's narrative. I wonder what her own, internal account would have been.

Life stories are like kaleidoscopes—they fall into different patterns depending on how you turn them. They are constructions, works of art just as novels are, only every single one of us creates them. We do best to remember that they are inventions. We can change them, not any which way we want to, but we can select one pattern over another, can shake the elements into different configurations. We are ongoing, always in the middle.

WHAT SHOULD A WRITER DO?

A CHILD OF THE 1960s and '70s, I've gravitated naturally to the progressive in politics, particularly once I became aware that being female had no small implications for my life. In college, trying to make sense of those implications—how to manage romances with men when I didn't always feel or want to be stereotypically feminine? how to deal with the fear of violence that came from simply walking down the streets near my dorm at night?—I voraciously worked my way through classic feminist texts by Simone de Beauvoir, Susan Brownmiller, Kate Millett, Betty Friedan, Shulamith Firestone, and others. On campus, student groups supported nuclear disarmament, the Nicaraguan Sandinistas, and the unionized Yale clerical and technical workers striking for better pay. College, in and out of the classroom, was an education in how power was misused against certain social groups and to oppose certain public goods.

Because I know what anyone knows who follows the

news, and because I react viscerally to injustice, I've always wrestled with my natural inclination to sit in a room reading or writing about imaginary people. With my natural desire for quiet and calm, my natural unease around strangers, my natural dislike of working in groups. Shouldn't I be out making things a little better for people who need it? I'm gratified when I receive the rare note from an appreciative reader, but it's hard to argue that giving someone a few hours of literary pleasure measures up against improving his or her work conditions, hourly wage, or access to good health care.

Middlemarch contains some distinct views on work and what makes it worthy, an ethical force in the world. Caleb Garth, a surveyor, builder, and land agent, is held up as the ideal workingman. He is honest to the bone and deplores laziness and corner cutting. The character of Caleb was partially based on George Eliot's father, who was also a land agent (someone who supervises the farming tenants of a large landowner). Though Eliot's relationship with her father was strained, she respected his work ethic and fair-minded pragmatism. Caleb Garth is perhaps a best-case version of Robert Evans. The Garths are poor because Caleb will never leave a job before every detail has been taken care of and because he refuses to charge more for what he does. Through her portrait of Caleb, Eliot clearly tells us what she believes makes work worthy: dedication, honesty, and good workmanship, a focus on the task rather than the financial reward for it. Lydgate is another such worker. Fred, we take it, comes to be one too. Characters in Eliot's other novels also embody this ideal, for instance Adam Bede, a rural carpenter, in the book bearing his name. These characters are not necessarily among her most highly educated; their knowledge is rooted in the land and in a tradition of craft. They are pointedly contrasted with others, such as Mr. Plymdale in *Middlemarch*, a fabrics merchant who has become wealthy using cheap dyes that rot his silks. And of course there is Bulstrode, whose philanthropy is built on a foundation of dishonorable business practices.

I'd like to believe Eliot would say that dedication to the craft of writing can be as honorable as the dedication to farming or furniture making. But she would probably reply that it is not so simple.

When *Middlemarch* was published, Eliot wrote in her journal, "No former book of mine has been received with more enthusiasm—not even Adam Bede, and I have received many deeply affecting assurances of its influence for good on individual minds. Hardly anything could have happened to me which I could regard as a greater blessing." Eliot had an agenda for her books; they were not merely distractions or intellectual stimulants. They were meant to *make people better*. We can be suspicious, today, of this motive for writing. It is probably one of the reasons that during the modernist period of the early twentieth century, Eliot came to seem fusty. The outstanding fiction of that period—Ford Madox Ford's *The Good Soldier*, Virginia Woolf's *Mrs. Dalloway* and *To the Lighthouse*, James Joyce's *Ulysses*—prioritized the rendering of consciousness and the perfection of form over the impulse to distinguish good from bad, virtue from evil. The sophisticated reader did not need to be condescended to by being taught ethics.

Other literary movements supplanted (and overlapped with) modernism, and moralism crept back in; it was just a question of *which* moralism. The critical and commercial success of authors such as Theodore Dreiser, Upton Sinclair, Sinclair Lewis, and John Dos Passos suggested that revealing the depravities of capitalism was the proper function of fiction. Starting in the 1960s, writers like Leonard Michaels and Philip Roth offered an anti-morality in which the old rules about sex and obedience to authority were tossed away. In every period, some of the works written under the sway of then-current social and political trends hold up as art, some do not. In twenty-five years it will be clearer what our own moralisms are. Some of the most enthusiastically received contemporary literature has been split between a painfully detailed attention to racial and sexual victimization (Colson Whitehead, Hanya Yanagihara) and a numb misanthropy (Ottessa Moshfegh, Michel Houellebecq). On the one hand we seem to be saying that investigating racial and sexual power is fiction's highest moral purpose, on the other that there is a perverse heroism in not caring much about morality at all.

The view of Eliot's work as didactic and overearnest was always unfair. To the engaged reader, her compassion and humor make dreariness impossible. Goodness has always been harder to write about than wickedness, and I find Eliot's attempt to dramatize it as thrilling as a high-wire act. So many other authors flee from this subject precisely because of the risk of sentimentalism, preachiness, and dishonesty. Eliot succeeds, and I am always shaking my head, asking: How does she do it?

Part of the answer is Eliot's commitment to observed truth. In an essay ("The Natural History of German Life") published shortly before her first attempts at fiction, she wrote that it was important for a novelist to show "not what are the motives and influences which the moralist thinks *ought* to act on the laborer or the artisan, but what are the motives and influences which *do* act on him." She is not afraid of showing "the peasant in all his coarse apathy, and the artisan in all his suspicious selfishness." Related to this is the fact that Eliot never loses herself inside her characters. This is remarkable, because she dives so completely into each psyche. But she always remembers to maintain a simultaneous view from the outside. The literary protagonists we find saccharine and unconvincing are those whom we are asked to see as they see themselves: good, gentle, and caring; or brave, protecting, rational, and strong. If an author presents anyone as those things and nothing else, we smell a rat. Eliot is interested in goodness that arises *within* the welter of selfishness, misperception, weakness, and fear that exists in every human being. She wants to know the conditions in which goodness can fight its way to the surface.

But what did she think this goodness consisted of?

In *The Mill on the Floss*, Eliot famously wrote: "We could never have loved the earth so well if we had had no childhood in it," invoking a child's unhurried hours with flowers and birds and familiar spots in nature, adding, "What novelty is worth that sweet monotony where everything is known, and *loved* because it is known?" For Eliot, goodness has its roots in the natural world and in the world of childhood. It's in childhood that we love spontaneously and with our whole being, and if we are fortunate, that impulse toward love is rewarded and strengthened rather than crimped or punished. (It is no accident that Mary and Fred have the most contented bond of any couple in *Middlemarch*, because it is one that began in childhood.) In nature we discover dramas beyond our own, and learn that the life outside us is as real as the life within. For Eliot, this recognition is the foundation of all morality.

Eliot's love of her own childhood landscape suffuses so many of her works of fiction: *Scenes of Clerical Life, Adam Bede, The Mill on the Floss, Middlemarch*. One has the sense that love and that landscape are the same for her. She, who has the reputation of being among the most intellectual of novelists, is one of the most grounded. From the crucible of childhood and a tactile experience of the world comes the development of empathy, and from empathy the desire to soothe the pain of others, and from this to what Eliot considers an even higher form of goodness: the willingness to *feel with* another person, even when one does not have power to remove the pain. The passages that bring me to the brink of tears each time I read *Middlemarch* are always the same. One I've mentioned before, when Harriet Bulstrode silently accepts and embraces her husband's shame. Another occurs when Lydgate reveals to Casaubon and Dorothea that Casaubon has degenerative heart disease. After Lydgate departs, Dorothea goes to her husband to comfort him, but he turns on her a "chill" glance; when she links her arm with his, he "kept his hands behind him and allowed her pliant arm to cling with difficulty against his rigid arm." This, after months of enduring Casaubon's coldness, finally drives her into a fury. For the first time she fully blames her husband for their unhappiness. She spends the entire day in her room, struggling with her thoughts and feelings. (I believe this scene must have been the inspiration for the famous one in Henry James's *Portrait of a Lady* in which, over the course of a long evening of introspection, Isabel Archer comes to understand the truth of her relationship with her husband.) Slowly, Dorothea works herself toward mastery of her rage. She waits until the late hour when Casaubon will be coming upstairs for bed, then walks out to greet him. She expects nothing, but wants to be better than her anger. Then:

When her husband stood opposite to her, she saw that his face was more haggard. He started slightly on seeing her, and she looked up at him beseechingly, without speaking.

"Dorothea!" he said, with a gentle surprise in his tone. "Were you waiting for me?"

"Yes, I did not like to disturb you."

"Come, my dear, come. You are young, and need not to extend your life by watching."

When the kind quiet melancholy of that speech fell on Dorothea's ears, she felt something like the thankfulness that might well up in us if we had narrowly escaped hurting a lamed creature. She put her hand into her husband's and they went along the broad corridor together.

Dorothea has traveled from the desire to hurt to the recognition that the one who has hurt her is as injured as she is, if in a different way. The concluding image of two flawed and suffering beings moving along together toward whatever is next: this, after all that has happened between these two characters, always touches me at a profound level. Casaubon will not really change. But Dorothea's willingness to feel for and with him creates relief and comfort for both of them. It brings out of her husband what capacity for tenderness he does possess. Lydgate, too, despite continually being bruised by Rosamond's deceptions and contempt for what he cares about most, manages to see through her eyes and extend her his sympathy more often than his anger. For all his casual sexism, Lydgate understands that he has his work, while Rosamond has only whatever status marriage and its trappings confer on her.

The kind of goodness Eliot writes about always involves specific acts of one-to-one recognition and effort. Dorothea, coming to Lydgate's defense when even his closest friends and colleagues hang back, chides them: "People glorify all sorts of bravery except the bravery they might show on behalf of their nearest neighbors."

While this kind of goodness seems simple and local, it is not at all easy. As Dorothea implies, justice at a distance is cheaper. One of Mr. Brooke's few definite activities as a magistrate is arguing to save men convicted of stealing property from the death penalty. This is a personal mission he has taken on. Yet he won't spend money to keep his own tenants in living conditions that might prevent them from being tempted to crime in the first place. In contrast, when Caleb Garth discovers that Bulstrode has withheld an inheritance from its rightful owner—this before the rest of the town learns the fact—he tells Bulstrode he can no longer work for him, even though his coming on as Bulstrode's manager has only very recently given the Garths some financial stability. Caleb's rejection of Bulstrode is neither angry nor jubilant, merely regretful. He believes the bad suffer more than the good do, so there's no need to pile on. He tells the banker he will say nothing to others, since he doesn't judge the other man and doesn't know the whole story. It's just that his unease makes it impossible to continue the employment.

Sometimes, I have to admit, *Middlemarch* makes me despair of ever being a decent human being. Can I imagine having the self-restraint, exquisite manners, generosity, and stoicism of its most beloved characters? Usually, no.

Luckily there is one character, clearly much admired by Eliot, who seems to get away with being a bit less good than Dorothea or Lydgate or Caleb Garth. This is Mary Garth. Mary has grown on me over the years. In the past I, like many of her co-characters, had a tendency to give her less than her due. She is easily overshadowed by the more strenuously aspiring and strenuously thwarted Dorothea.

We first meet Mary when Rosamond visits her at

Stone Court, Peter Featherstone's estate. Mary, recall, is Featherstone's nurse-companion. Rosamond and Mary know each other from their school days and of course because of Mary's continuing friendship with Fred. Rosamond has come because she knows Lydgate has been making house calls to Featherstone, and she wants the inside story on the handsome new doctor in town. The narrator gives us the contrast between the two girls: the slim, fashionable Rosamond, with "eyes of heavenly blue," who strikes everyone, especially men, as "an angel." But "Mary Garth, on the contrary, had the aspect of an ordinary sinner: she was brown; her curly dark hair was rough and stubborn; her stature was low; and it would not be true to declare, in satisfactory antithesis, that she had all the virtues."

Mary has a streak of bitterness, Eliot tells us, because her lot has been harder than that of many of the girls she grew up with. As a child, she was a "hoyden," and she has a temper. But she is intelligent and has been well educated by her mother, who works giving lessons to children despite having six of her own. Honesty, with herself and others, is "Mary's reigning virtue," and she has a sense of humor. Catching sight of herself and Rosamond in a mirror, she laughs that she is "a brown patch" next to her old friend. She is aware of her imperfections, both physical and temperamental, and embraces them humbly. (Eliot is fond of those with this combination of humility and self-acceptance. Of the Reverend Farebrother, she says that his belief that he is not unusual is the most unusual thing about him.)

Mary also has standards, as we see in an encounter between her and Fred where, after he reminds her of his desire to marry her, she pretty plainly tells him he's too immature to be her husband. One reason for her boldness may be that she is used to living simply and knows she can support herself as a governess or companion if necessary. Rosamond believes she *must* have certain furniture, clothing, and social opportunities. Therefore she must marry. Mary has no such airs, and so there's no reason for her to settle for someone she isn't sure she loves and respects.

Mary is rather a relief when I consider how far I am from any of the models of good behavior in *Middlemarch*. Even she is a lot to aspire to: in her shoes I would spend most of my time with the surly, abusive Featherstone raging or weeping. I would throw myself on the floor and insist my parents bring me home. I might well then marry the first passable man who came along. Mary has a lot more forbearance. She has the right kind of self-control: far-thinking, not masochistic.

But she is also assertive and judgmental, and not sorry about it. We see that this side of her comes from her mother, who is also sharp-tongued.

Part of me, as I've said, has always felt I should be a Dorothea, and wondered if I would ever find that less impossible. In my fifties, though, I see her less as an attainable model than as a beautiful ideal, Eliot's attempt to persuasively embody goodness in human form. Bernard J. Paris, a literary scholar who wrote a 1965 book entitled *Experiments in Life: George Eliot's Quest for Values*, followed this up nearly forty years later with another book, *Rereading George Eliot*, in which he renounced his previously glowing view of Eliot's moral philosophy. Life experience and psychotherapy had since convinced him that while Dorothea, Lydgate, and other characters in Eliot's fiction are implicitly lauded for their acts of egolessness, they are actually engaged in pointlessly self-destructive behavior. They become "enslaved by the wishes of others." Eliot "fails to discriminate between the legitimate needs of others and their unreasonable claims," a failure that "is usually obscured by plot and rhetoric." Paris finds the self-denial of these characters "compulsive."[10]

Paris definitely has a point—I've noted earlier that Eliot avoids facing the consequences of Dorothea's disastrous devotion to Casaubon by having him die of heart disease. Paris hypothesizes that Eliot was so preoccupied with notions of duty and self-sacrifice in her fiction because of guilt over choices made at certain turning points in her life, for instance when she refused to embrace traditional religion despite her father's protests, and when she decided to live openly with a married man. This theory is unprovable but does make me interrogate my own readings of Dorothea and Lydgate. Maybe guilt over my own comfort and autonomy— my unwillingness to live my life only for others—has made me overidealize them. (I certainly know readers who find Dorothea intensely annoying rather than inspiring.) Paris sees Dorothea's saintliness as a kind of self-aggrandizement, and not just at the start of the novel. He sees Lydgate's surrendering to Rosamond's shallow demands as evidence of a desperate and pathetic need to be needed.

All good novels contain contradictions when it comes to values; they wouldn't be interesting if they didn't. I nod vigorously at Paris's insights, but I still see a magnificence in Dorothea's and Lydgate's characters. As I get older, Eliot's worldview scores some palpable victories with me. Recently, two good friends failed to respond for many days to important (to me) emails. Normally this would have blindsided me with worry and anger. I would have started to tell myself that my friends didn't value me. Like Dorothea in her boudoir counting the hurts received from her husband, I would have begun to think of ways to make my upset known, or to self-protectively withdraw my affections. This time, I simply figured there were reasons for the silence that had nothing to do with me. I believe more now in the basic decency of people. Even when someone behaves badly toward me, I am more able to let it go—not because I've become more saintly but because it seems more evident that I'm not the centering flame of every situation. What made me police my boundaries so rigidly in the past were my pride and my fear of being taken advantage of, not some ineradicable badness. In this understanding—and self-forgiveness—I see Eliot's attitudes at work: we want to behave well not to earn ethical gold stars but because it is more consonant with the way the world actually works. At times I have had more compassion for my fictional characters than for the real people in my life—have viewed them with more indulgence—but maybe the former, nurtured by Eliot's example, paved the way for the latter.

•

Eliot did not think morality ended with the interpersonal. She was interested in the political activism and reform movements of her time and earlier. The novel she wrote right before *Middlemarch—Felix Holt, the Radical—*takes place in exactly the same era but deals more head-on with politicking and debates around the Reform Bill of 1832, which created fairer voting districts and extended the franchise. In *Felix Holt* we see shady electioneering practices, such as buying votes with alcohol, and there is an election riot. *Romola*, the novel preceding *Felix Holt*, covers political unrest in late fifteenth-century Florence. *Daniel Deronda*, Eliot's last novel, deals with the birth of Zionism. And the struggles of Maggie Tulliver in *The Mill on the Floss*, Dorothea in *Middlemarch*, and Gwendolen Harleth and Princess Halm-Eberstein in *Daniel Deronda* all testify to the need for legal and social changes that would release nineteenth-century women from dependence on fathers, brothers, and husbands.

But Eliot never believed in radical solutions to the status quo. She was suspicious of any change that too abruptly altered settled ways of being. She knew that tradition and stability nurture communities and felt that while changes might be welcome or needed, they were most successful when they came gradually. "The bent of my mind is conservative rather than destructive," she wrote in an 1868 letter.[11] The passage brings me back to a conversation I had in college with friends who were involved in the Committee in Solidarity with the People of El Salvador, a group opposing the US government's 1980s interventions there. Some of those friends argued that they would be justified in committing violence in the service of that opposition. Their analysis, as I listened, seemed so logical; I had trouble putting my finger on the flaw—and yet I shrank from their conclusion. I felt guilty that I shrank from it. Was I content to let wrongdoing go on and on? Did I just not care enough? In *Middlemarch*, Eliot articulates what I inchoately felt: "There is no general doctrine which is not capable of eating out our morality if unchecked by the deep-seated habit of direct fellow-feeling with individual fellow-men." If I'd remembered that line, I might have pleaded this case: that acts in the name of morality must always be constrained by reality testing and ethical qualms. That it is too easy to convince ourselves that we can decide for other people what kinds of pain and harm are acceptable. Yes, I might have added, outrageous injustices are occurring at every moment in every part of the world. But addressing each, or any, with violence is not the answer. If we had to see what violence wreaks on both the guilty and the innocent, if we could know each victim as someone's brother, sister, mother, father, or dear friend, we would never agree to it. (For the record, I don't believe that anyone in the room that day was ever involved in a violent act or plan.)

Perhaps because her progressive ideals ran up against her fears about radical change, Eliot never openly participated in any political movement, nor did she proselytize for any specific positions. According to one scholar, she "disliked embroiling herself in controversial issues, because she did not feel wise enough and because she disliked being forced to disagree with others."[12] That sums me up as well. I have tried—and hated—phoning voters and knocking on doors to get people to agree with something I believe. I cringe at school board meetings when speakers grow hot and combative. I feel very strongly about some matters (the right to abortion, the right of free speech, making it easier for citizens to vote). But whenever I try to put my energies toward activism, I become more and more miserable until I eventually flee, ashamed, back to merely intellectual engagement (otherwise known as the endless reading of magazine think pieces). Social anxiety? Mild agoraphobia? Possibly. I still do this kind of low-level political work from time to time, and I also write checks—it just never seems like enough. Eliot could rationalize her nonparticipation with her belief that her novels were improvements for the soul. Can I?

Not really. And that's a problem, because not only do I not see my novels as moral improvements, I don't see fiction, period, as an inherently moral pursuit. I don't think it's immoral; nor do I believe it's frivolous. For anyone who is serious about it, the writing of fiction takes enormous dedication and craft. It requires a battle for psychological honesty, precision, and perspective. Excessive self-love is toxic to it. In this sense, perhaps, writing is as honorable as Caleb Garth's building and farming activities. But stories and novels themselves are way too ambiguous to be held up as morally improving or instructing. I don't even like the idea of trying to improve other people. What would give me the right to do so? I'm no moral exemplar, and in any case I don't think morality is so easily passed from one hand to another. Eliot managed to create powerful stories of moral struggle and enlightenment, but they weren't simple, and she was the exception proving the rule that moral instruction, for a novelist, is a dangerous goal. If there's any moral agenda I can claim as a writer, it's the more circumspect one Eliot articulated in a letter to her friend Charles Bray: "The only effect I ardently long to produce by my writings, is that those who read them should be better able to *imagine* and to *feel* the pains and the joys of those who differ from themselves in everything but the broad fact of being struggling erring human creatures."[13]

This I can acknowledge as an impetus: the desire to make others feel. In my case, that desire may be more selfish than Eliot's: what I want my readers to feel is often something I have felt too alone with. The situations in my fiction are rarely autobiographical, but I have arranged them to trigger the experience of some sort of emotion that is. If I am encouraging readers to feel, it is so that *I* can be less lonely, not because it's necessarily going to do something for them. And yet sometimes I do get a message from a reader suggesting that he or she has received something from me. Perhaps my willingness (compulsion?) to risk shame and vulnerability, to explore feelings and impulses in myself that I may fear or hate, gives reassurance to others that their own inner life is not unmentionable. Does fiction work somewhat like Adam Smith's invisible hand—when we each write for our own selfish ends, something good for all of us results? This would fly very much in the face of George Eliot's philosophy, but it's probably closer to my experience.

Maybe I am still stuck on the lower rungs of Eliot's

hierarchy of moral activity, the rung of nature and the tactile. After my first child was born, my decision to leave my magazine job was driven by something akin to Eliot's feelings about being grounded in the rhythms and materiality of early life. I didn't live on or near a farm and there weren't even a lot of trees and flowers around, but the job of taking care of an infant is thoroughly physical, and I wanted to experience that fully. I wanted to nurse, to change the diapers, to hold my child when it cried, to smell its smells and feel its skin against me. I wanted to bring the first spoon of solid food to its mouth, see the first tooth come in, guide the first steps. I didn't want to do this a few hours of the day while I was rushing to get to work or after I got home, already tired out. I wanted to do it on the more leisurely, relaxed schedule that would help me tune in. To know my child, it seemed to me, I had to be there most of the time, and through this being there my love for my child would take shape. I am not saying that what I did is right for anyone else or even that it was surely the best thing for my two children, just that it was right for me at the time. Maybe because my own life had never felt that connected to the immanent world, I wanted to experience that through my own mothering. My decision to stay home, to "invest" in my kids, was part narcissism, part self-sacrifice (and part upper-middle-class privilege). It was done for them, and for me, and to enable my writing. Whatever the outcome, it was an attempt at something higher, outward facing, and future embracing.

As suggested in "The Natural History of German Life," Eliot did see value in the aspect of art that merely reflected reality rather than sought to improve readers. If goodness and hope are not the particular truths a writer is interested in, she simply needs to show the ones that do capture her as faithfully as she can. And, I'd like to ask here, isn't beauty also something to take into account? The beauty of language is a gift in and of itself, as a beautiful vase or piece of music is a gift and can solace us. A sentence that possesses music, clarity, and honest feeling can stop me, make me read again, cause me to shiver with delight. Maybe providing that experience to someone, somewhere, a handful of times is as much goodness as I can hope to accomplish. At a gathering of writers working together to defeat Trump in the 2020 election, Siri Hustvedt, one of the organizers, talked about how literary writing is one-to-one speech, one voice speaking to one reader at a time. It is the opposite, she said, of our inescapable mass media and of the simplified, hammered-in-via-repetition language that demagogues use. Good writing is slow in its effects. Yet in a strange way its inefficiency, its one-to-oneness, offers hope for forming communities based on emotional honesty and critical thinking. Another paradox about literature is that each individual writer draws on and is shaped by the long history of books that came before. Individuality and community fuse in the work of fiction making and reading.

I remember those times, in my midteens through midtwenties especially, when, as I've described, the sentences in novels held me in place, made it possible to move through the hours, channeled my anxieties, and reawakened the experience of hope, laughter, empathy, and joy. Is that such a small thing?

In the fall of 2001, when the World Trade Center fell, I happened to be in the middle of reading *Anna Karenina*. In the subsequent weeks, my terror and my preoccupation with the implications of the attack for my small children often made it impossible for me to read anything but the newspaper. But during other hours, Tolstoy's novel was precisely what I needed. The narrator he employs in *Anna Karenina*, like the one Eliot employs in *Middlemarch*, is a sense-making machine. Moving from sentence to sentence I found an order and stability that was reassuring, even though I knew that when I raised my head from the novel I would be back in a frightening, unpredictable world. The order of *Anna Karenina* did not feel false or obsolete. It did not matter that the world in it was a bygone world. I wasn't looking to the novel to promise me that everything would be all right at the start of the twenty-first century in the United States of America. I simply needed to be bodily reminded—for the rhythm of sentences is a bodily experience—that order of some kind, any kind, was possible. When the surprise of Trump's election arrived in November 2016, I was in the middle of Margot Livesey's novel *Mercury*. Another sense-making machine. And during March, April, May, and June 2020, I worked my way, under Yiyun Li's leadership, through *War and Peace*. In mid-June, after we finished the book, 650 of us joined a Zoom event to hear Li discuss it. The chat line scrolled rapidly with expressions of deep gratitude for the experience of reading the novel during this time.

At the end of *Middlemarch*, we learn that Dorothea, now married to Will Ladislaw and living in London, has a child who will inherit Mr. Brooke's estate. Dorothea never performs any great acts of saintliness or philanthropy that the narrator finds worth telling us about; we hear that the good things she does "were not widely visible." But she continues to affect those around her in a way that is "incalculably diffusive: for the growing good of the world is partly dependent on unhistoric acts; and that things are not so ill with you and me as they might have been, is half owing to the number who lived faithfully a hidden life, and rest in unvisited tombs."

The gorgeous melody of these sentences never fails to stir me. The work I am best fitted to do may be this: to strive to fashion stories that might keep someone else, someone I don't even know, pinned to well-being for a few hours, a few days. I hope my work has served in that way, or will. I know what it is like to be saved by sentences.

ACKNOWLEDGMENTS

Thank you to Robert Lasner and Elizabeth Clementson, who created the wonderful Bookmarked series and invited me to take part in it. Thank you to Robin Black, Therese Eiben, Jon Michaud, and Joanne Serling, whose feedback helped me write a stronger book, and to Anne Horowitz, whose copyediting always makes me look better. Thank you to David Chien and to Rebecca Mead's *My Life in Middlemarch* for insights. Thank you to Anna Stein for always supporting me as I chase my various interests.

NOTES

1. Stanford Literary Lab, "Style at the Scale of the Sentence," *n+1*, no. 17 (Fall 2013): 111, https://nplusonemag.com/issue-17/essays/style-at-the-scale-of-the-sentence/.

2. Lewis to Arthur Greeves, March 29, 1931, in *The Collected Letters of C. S. Lewis, Vol. 1: Family Letters 1905–1931* (Grand Rapids, MI: Zondervan, 2009).

3. Even in third person, the narrator of a novel is never identical with the author. In these pages, I often refer to something that "Eliot" says or does or thinks. I do this because it feels stiff and ponderous to say "the narrator" all the time. But unless I am talking about the biographical Eliot, when I use her name I really mean the ingenious persona the author has invented to tell her tale.

4. Joan Bennett, *George Eliot: Her Mind and Her Art* (Cambridge: Cambridge University Press, 1966), 85.

5. Jill Lepore, "The History of Loneliness," *New Yorker*, April 6, 2020, https://www.newyorker.com/magazine/2020/04/06/the-history-of-loneliness. The historian whose work is referenced is Fay Bound Alberti.

6. Rebecca Mead, *My Life in Middlemarch* (New York: Crown, 2014), 136. The remark appears originally in John Cross, *George Eliot's Life*, vol. 3 (New York: Harper & Brothers; Project Gutenberg, 2013), section 306, http://www.gutenberg.org/files/43045/43045-h/43045-h.htm.

7. The book was *Das Leben Jesu* (*Life of Jesus*), published in 1835 by David Friedrich Strauss, a Protestant theologian. Eliot's translation was published in 1846.

8. Paula Marantz Cohen, "Why Read George Eliot?" *American Scholar* (Spring 2006), https://theamericanscholar.org/why-read-george-eliot/.

9. Virginia Woolf, "George Eliot," in *The Common Reader, First Series,* Harcourt Brace Jovanovich, 1984, pp. 162-172.

10. Bernard J. Paris, *Rereading George Eliot: Changing Responses to Her Experiments in Life* (Albany: State University of New York Press, 2003), 2, 5–6, and 40.

11. Eliot to Clifford Allbutt, August 1868, in *Middlemarch: A Norton Critical Edition*, ed. Bert G. Hornback (New York: W. W. Norton, 1977), 594.

12. June Skye Szirotny, "Why George Eliot Was Not a Political Activist," *Journal of International Women's Studies* 13, no. 3 (2012): 184–93, https://vc.bridgew.edu/jiws/vol13/iss3/13/.

13. Eliot to Charles Bray, July 5, 1859, in *Middlemarch: A Norton Critical Edition*, ed. Bert G. Hornback (New York: W. W. Norton, 1977), 591.

OTHER
BOOKMARKED TITLES

Mario Puzo's *The Godfather*
by Atar Hadari (forthcoming)

Mary Gaitskill's *Bad Behavior*
by JoAnna Novak (forthcoming)

Virginia Woolf's *Mrs. Dalloway*
by Robin Black

James Baldwin's *Another Country*
by Kim McLarin

Truman Capote's *In Cold Blood*
by Justin St. Germain

Vladimir Nabokov's *Speak, Memory*
by Sven Birkerts

William Stoner and the Battle for the Inner Life
by Steve Almond

Stephen King's "The Body"
by Aaron Burch

Raymond Carver's *What We Talk About When We Talk About Love*
by Brian Evenson

(For a complete series list, go to
https://www.igpub.com/category/titles/bookmarked/)